The Photographic
Dictionary of Soccer

The Photo
Dictionary

graphic
of Soccer

by Tim Considine

WARNER BOOKS

A Warner Communications Company

**The Photographic
Dictionary of Soccer**

WARNER BOOKS EDITION ·

ISBN 0-446-87953-3

Cover photos by Tim Considine

Designed by the Author,
Thomas Nozkowski and William Giersbach

Warner Books, Inc.,
75 Rockefeller Plaza,
New York, N.Y. 10019

 A Warner Communications Company

Printed in the United States of America

Not associated with Warner Press, Inc.,
of Anderson, Indiana

First Printing: March, 1979

10 9 8 7
6 5 4
3 2
1

The photo collages starting on page 197
are by the author and Kenny Blustajn.

TO PELE

The King

The Black Pearl

God of the Stadiums

and now

The Pied Piper of American Soccer

Acknowledgements

The author would like to thank the many kind people who helped make this book possible, including Tom Craig, for his invaluable editorial assistance in preparing the manuscript; David Keith, for the hours spent in the darkroom developing and printing photographs for the book; Rita Eichinger, for her assistance in the collection and typing of facts and materials from all over the United States; Willie Hunt and Kevin Considine, for their photographic assistance in the field; and Peri Winkler, for her counsel and support

The author would also like to thank Ursula Melendi and John Bragg of the United States Soccer Federation, Jim Trecker of the North American Soccer League, Haskell Cohen of the American Soccer League, Hans Stierle of the American Youth Soccer Organization, and the member clubs of both the ASL and the NASL for their kind assistance in providing materials for the book.

And finally, the author would like to thank the coaches, officials, and players who patiently answered question after question, and whose enthusiasm and encouragement greatly assisted the completion of this book.

Introduction

After a hundred years of trying, soccer is a major sport in the United States. While the game has been played by dedicated enthusiasts since it was introduced here in the 1860s by British sailors and merchants, it was not until the mid-1970s that soccer was able to shed its image as a foreign or immigrant's game and enter the mainstream of American sport alongside baseball, basketball, and American football, itself a derivation of soccer. Now it seems that one seldom can pass a park, playground, or schoolyard without seeing soccer balls being kicked around, or open a magazine or turn on the television without being sold on the virtues of some product by one of the new soccer heroes—proof positive in this society that soccer has arrived.

The turning point came on June 15, 1975, the day that Pele, the legendary Brazilian superstar, came out of retirement to play his first game for an American professional soccer team, the New York Cosmos of the North American Soccer League. With the presence of the most popular athlete in the world, the Cosmos, the league, and American soccer gained instant credibility. Television and the news media suddenly took interest and began to spread the message. In the 2½ years that followed, millions of Americans were introduced to soccer by the greatest player in the history of the game as he shattered all existing attendance records and led his team to a national championship and world recognition. By the time Pele played his last game as a Cosmo on October 1, 1977, adding yet another "miracle goal" to his record total on national television, and in front of 76,000 rain-soaked diehards, the nation had adopted soccer.

It is the American youth who benefited the most, for they have taken to the freedom and simplicity of soccer. Here is a game that places no great advantage in size, or shape, or gender, but rather stresses skill, condition, and imagination. All that is needed to play soccer is a ball and a reasonably flat area. With the openness and easy accessibility of the game, and such models to emulate as the incomparable Pele and the other world-class players who followed him here, as well as America's own soccer heroes, it is not surprising that youth soccer has grown so much in so little time. Already in many states more kids play organized soccer than Little League baseball or Pop Warner football.

With the "new" sport has come a new language. The modern-day sports fan or parent must now be familiar with such terms as bicycle kick, cross, mark, header, nutmeg, sweeper, and trap, as well as know the decidedly different soccer meanings for such familiar American words as dribble, tackle, and pitch.

This book attempts to define soccer photographically essentially in the first section, which is a simple overview of the sport for the new enthusiast; and specifically in the second section, where 178 soccer terms and expressions are defined, illustrated, and whenever possible, demonstrated photographically. The third section contains the official international rules or *laws* of soccer. In the fourth section a list of milestones in American soccer is followed by a complete photo index.

The text will be most helpful to those new or just learning the sport, particularly in the first section, which is designed to be used as a spectators' guide or primer. The photographs are for all who love the game of soccer. Together they comprise a collector's edition of game-action photographs of some of the greatest players in the sport, from the incomparable Pele and other world-class players to America's own budding soccer stars, all demonstrating, defining, and celebrating the fastest-growing sport in America, soccer.

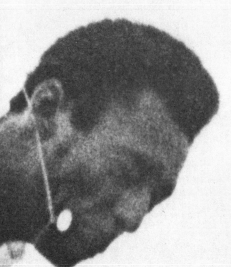

Part One: A Soccer Primer

A soccer pitch is roughly the size of an American football field or slightly larger, with a goal at each end.

15

There are eleven players on a side: one goalkeeper and ten field players called defenders, midfielders, and forwards or strikers. The names denote their primary responsibilities.

The referee controls the game. He starts and stops the match, keeps the official time (ninety minutes played in two forty-five-minute halfs), and enforces the rules of the game.

The goalkeeper is the only player allowed to touch the ball with the arms or hands, and then only when he is inside the marked penalty area.

All other field players must use their head…

their body...

their feet or legs to control the ball and move it toward the opponent's goal.

21

They may run with the ball...

fake, feint, or dribble it past opponents.

They may loft a pass across the field to a speeding teammate.

Opposing players may challenge for possession…

or tackle the ball.

charge...

push...

kick...

strike…

trip...

33

hold or otherwise obstruct an opponent.

Players may not engage in dangerous or unsportsmanlike conduct. These infractions are called fouls.

Depending on the foul and where it is committed, the referee may award possession to the fouled team, award a penalty shot to the fouled team, officially caution and report a player, or if necessary even eject a player from the game.

38   **When the ball crosses over the goal line wide of the goal, a goal kick is awarded to the defending team if the ball last touched an attacker.**

If the ball last touched a defender, the attacking team will be awarded a corner kick.

A corner kick is a scoring opportunity for the attacking team and a special threat to defenders. The ball is usually lofted into the area in front of the goal mouth...

where it can be headed goalward by an attacking teammate.

When the ball goes out of bounds on a sideline a throw-in is awarded to the team opposing the player to last touch the ball. A linesman (one on each sideline) makes the determination.

Linesmen also keep watch for another infraction that can stop play or even disqualify a goal: offside. There must be two opponents between an attacking player without the ball and the goal at the time the ball is played by an attacking teammate. When the linesman's flag is up an attacking player is offside. The defending team is then awarded possession of the ball.

There are many fouls that the referee does not call because no advantage was gained by the foul. To stop play would actually penalize the victim of the foul by removing an advantage. In soccer a momentary advantage could mean time to kick the ball downfield to a teammate racing toward the goal…

or it could mean two steps into an open space behind the last defender—a chance.

But the point of the game is to put the ball into the opponent's net—a GOAL!

Part Two:
The Photographic Dictionary of Soccer

ADVANTAGE RULE
Option in the rules of soccer enabling the referee to disregard a foul if a stoppage of play would take away an advantage held by the fouled player.

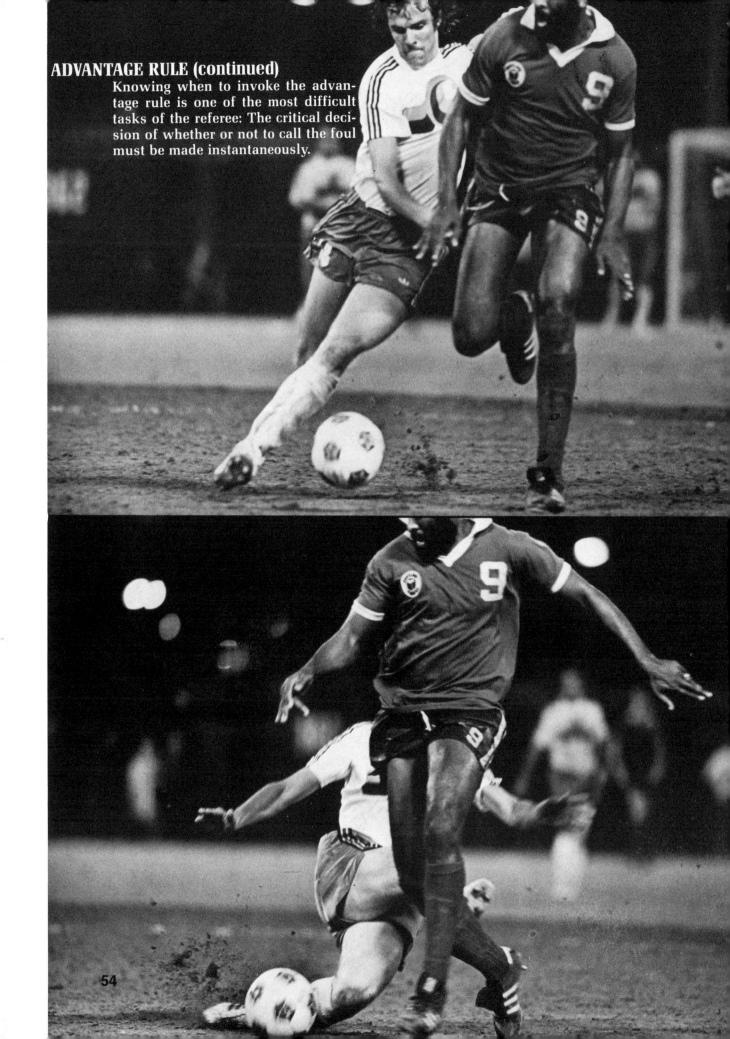

ADVANTAGE RULE (continued)

Knowing when to invoke the advantage rule is one of the most difficult tasks of the referee: The critical decision of whether or not to call the foul must be made instantaneously.

54

AIR BALL
A ball that is in the air, or in flight.

ASL

American Soccer League, older of the two major professional leagues in the United States, founded in 1934.

In 1978 the ASL numbered ten franchises split into two divisions.

EASTERN DIVISION

New Jersey Americans

Cleveland Cobras

Connecticut Yankees

New York Eagles

New York Apollos

Indianapolis Daredevils

Pennsylvania Stoners

Columbus Eleven

WESTERN DIVISION

California Sunshine

Sacramento Spirits

Los Angeles Skyhawks

Los Angeles Lazers

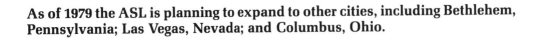
Las Vegas Seagulls

Golden Gate Gales

As of 1979 the ASL is planning to expand to other cities, including Bethlehem, Pennsylvania; Las Vegas, Nevada; and Columbus, Ohio.

ASSOCIATION FOOTBALL

The official international name of soccer, called football everywhere but in the United States and Canada.

AYSO

American Youth Soccer Organization. Founded in 1964 in California, AYSO is the largest youth soccer organization in the United States, with programs for boys and girls between five and eighteen years old. In keeping with the registered slogan "Everyone Plays," specific rules require balanced teams and that each player on a team play at least one half of every game. The AYSO now operates in twenty-one states.

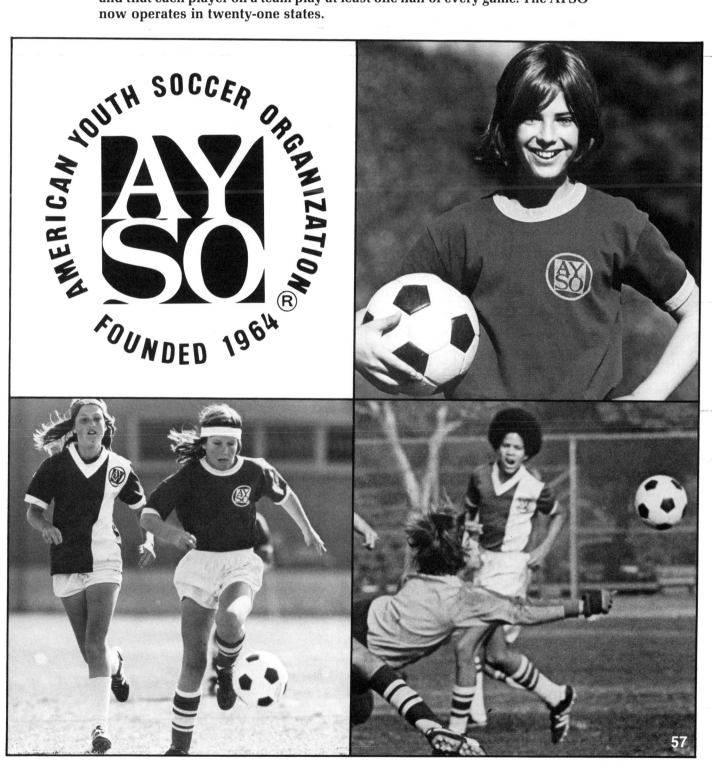

BACK

A defender who plays on the backline and assists the goalkeeper by blocking, intercepting, and turning back attacks by opposing forwards. Also DEFENDER.

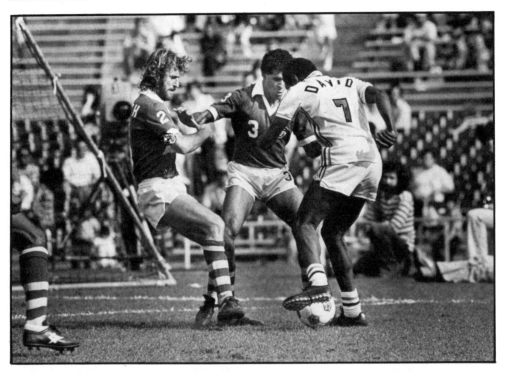

BACK-HEEL KICK

Technique whereby the heel is used to kick the ball backward.

BANANA KICK

Technique whereby the ball is kicked and made to spin so as to bend or curve in flight, as around a wall of defenders.

BICYCLE KICK

Technique whereby a player leaps almost upside down to perform an overhead kick of an air ball. Also OVERHEAD VOLLEY.

BLIND-SIDE RUNNING

Technique whereby a player without the ball runs into an attacking space behind or unseen by the distracted defenders.

BLOCK TACKLE

Technique whereby the front part of the body is used to block the ball to stop an attacking player. Also FRONT TACKLE.

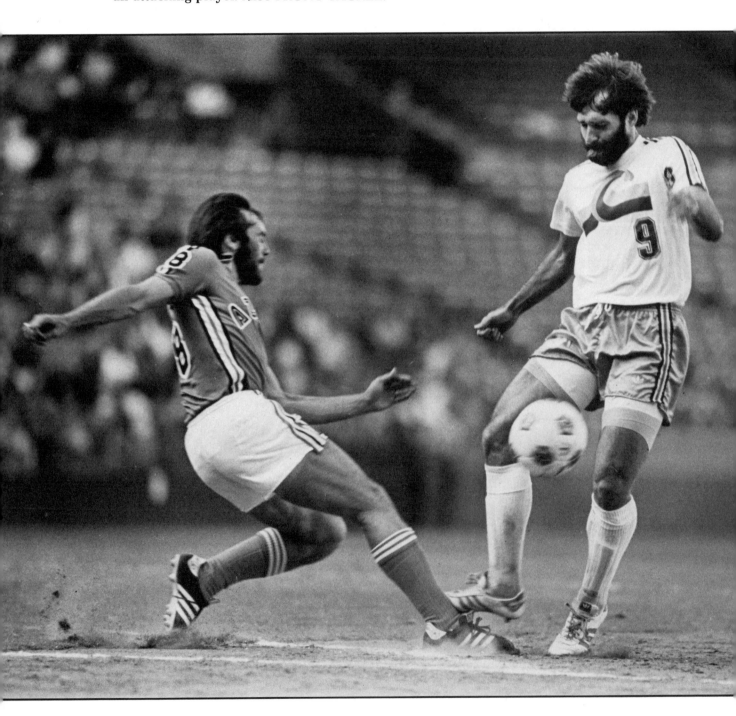

BOOKING

See CAUTION.

BOUNCE BALL
See DROP BALL.

BRING THE BALL DOWN
The use of any of the various techniques of trapping and controlling an air ball until it reaches the ground.

BUILD UP

An attack and the way it is mounted and supported by teamwork.

CAPS

A term of merit awarded to players who participate in international games between teams that represent nations. In some countries a ceremonial tasseled cap is given to each player for every game.

CAUTION

An official warning by the referee to a player signified by the showing of a yellow card. Also BOOKING: YELLOW CARD.

CENTER

To kick or play the ball from the side or sideline area toward attacking players in the center of the playing field, usually near or in front of the goal area; also CROSS.

CENTER BACK

A central defender. See FORMATIONS for illustration.

CENTER CIRCLE

A circle with a ten-yard radius marked around the actual center of the playing field. See PITCH for illustration.

CENTER FORWARD

The central attacking player on the forward line. Also STRIKER. See FORMATIONS for illustration.

CENTER HALF

Originally the center player on the middle line of the classic 2-3-5 "Pyramid" formation with two defenders, three midfielders, and five forwards. With the introduction of the 3-4-3 formation in the late twenties and the thirties the center half was moved back to a position between the two fullbacks to defend against the attacking center forward. See FORMATIONS for illustration.

CENTER SPOT

A mark made to designate the actual center of the playing field halfway between the goal lines and the sidelines. See PITCH for illustration.

CHANCE
An opportunity to shoot at the goal.

CHANGE
To kick or play the ball from one sideline across the field to a teammate at or near the opposite sideline. Also SWITCH.

CHARGING
Bodily contact, usually shoulder to shoulder.

CHARGING (continued)

An infraction unless at the time of the charge both players are going for a ball that is within playing distance.

CHARGING (continued)
An infraction from behind unless the opponent is obviously obstructing the charging player from the ball.

67

CHEST TRAP
Technique whereby the chest is used to stop and control an air ball.

CHIP
A kicking technique whereby the ball is lifted high for a short distance, usually over an opponent. Also FLIGHT, LOFT.

CLEAR To kick or head the ball away from the goal-mouth area, out of danger.

CLEARING OFF THE LINE

To kick or head the ball off the goal line, the goalkeeper may also use his hands to knock the ball away.

CORNER FLAG

A small flag atop a post of not less than five feet in length placed at each corner of the playing field. See PITCH for illustration.

CORNER KICK

A direct free kick taken from within the corner arc awarded to the attacking team when the defender is the last to touch a ball that crosses the goal line out of play. Also CORNER.

CORNER-KICK ARC
A small arc with a meter radius marked in each corner of the playing field enclosing the area in which corner kicks are taken. Also CORNER ARC. See PITCH for illustration.

CROSS

A high centering pass from the side or sideline area sent into the penalty area near or in front of the goal making it possible for attacking teammates to shoot at the goal. Also CENTER.

CROSSBAR

A horizontal bar that marks the top of the goal between the two goalposts. The bar is eight yards in length and eight feet above the ground.

DANGEROUS PLAY

Any action by a player that the referee considers dangerous or likely to cause injury to a teammate or opponent.

DEAD BALL

A ball out of play. This occurs when the ball crosses a goal line or a sideline, or after a stoppage of play.

DEFENDER

A player on the back line whose primary responsibility is to assist the goalkeeper with defense, turning back attacking opponents either by denying them the opportunity for a clear shot at the goal or by blocking the ball and clearing it to safety.

DRAGGING THE BALL BACK

Sudden use of the foot to bring the ball closer.

DRIBBLE

To maneuver through opponents using the feet to tap, push, and control the ball.

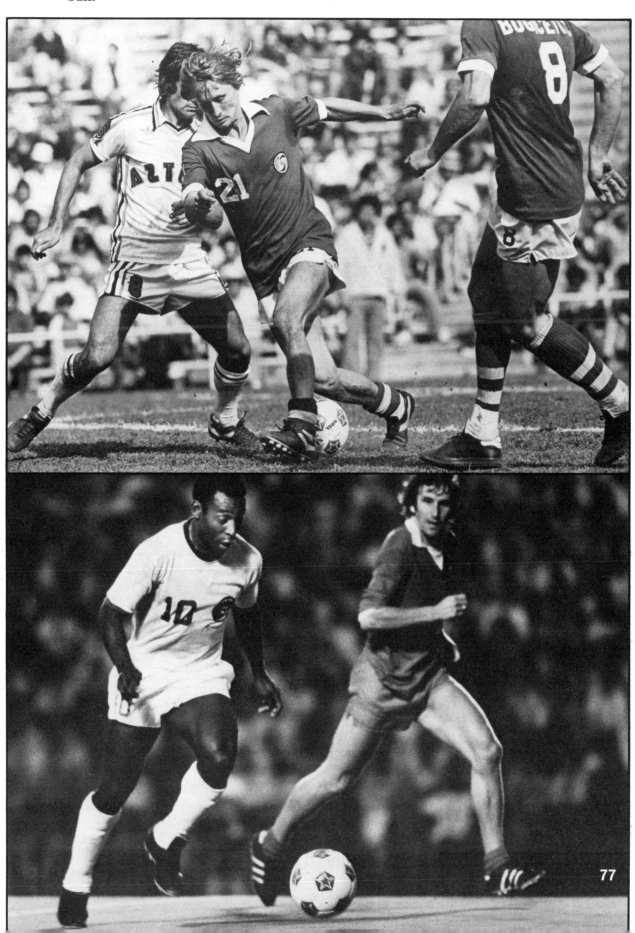

DROP BALL

The method by which the referee restarts the game that has been stopped due to serious injury, outside influence, or too many men on the field. The referee drops the ball between two opposing players. Neither player may touch the ball until it touches the ground.

DROP KICK

Goalkeeper's technique whereby the ball is dropped and kicked down the field just as it rises from the ground.

DROP PASS

The technique whereby an attacking player in full stride steps over the ball and backheels it to a trailing teammate or simply leaves it for a trailing teammate.

DROP ZONE

An unguarded space into which the ball is played to link up with oncoming teammates.

DUMMY

A fake or feint to cause an opponent to commit to a course of action.

EJECTION

When a player is officially thrown out of the game by the referee for a serious infraction. Also RED CARD, BEING SENT OFF.

ENCROACHMENT

An infraction whereby a player comes too close to the ball (within ten yards) in the case of a free kick, kickoff, or corner kick, interferes with the movement of a goalkeeper, or interferes with a throw-in.

FACE OFF

See DROP BALL.

FAR POST

The goalpost farthest from where the ball is being played.

FIFA

The Federation of International Football Associations; the international governing body of soccer, founded in 1904. Based in Zurich, Switzerland, FIFA has a membership of 154 nations.

FIFTY-FIFTY BALL

A free ball in play that opponents have an equal chance of playing.

FINISH

To shoot at the goal.

FIRST TIME

A moving ball that is passed, shot, or cleared on the first touch without trapping or controlling the ball. Also ONE TOUCH.

FIST

The goalkeeper's use of the clenched hand to punch a dangerous air ball away from the goal. Also PUNCH SAVE.

FLICK-ON HEADER

The use of the head to strike an air ball in such a way as to keep the ball moving in its original direction.

FLIGHT

To kick a ball up into the air. Also LOFT, CHIP.

FOOT TRAP

Use of the foot to stop and control a moving ball whether in the air or on the ground.

FORMATIONS

Different alignments of players on the soccer field at the time of a kickoff, usually expressed by a series of three digits indicating the number of players at the defense, midfield, and forward positions.

The 2-3-5 or Pyramid is considered the classic formation.

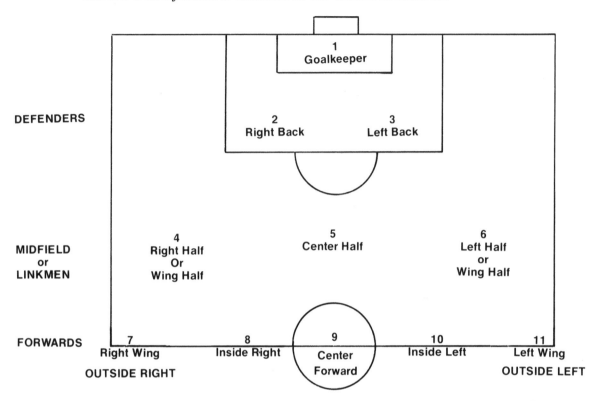

The first major change was the 3-4-3, or W-M formation. Note how the two inside forwards, No. 8 and No. 10, move back to the midfield, and the center half, No. 5, moves back to become a third fullback. While actually a center back, the position is still sometimes referred to as center half.

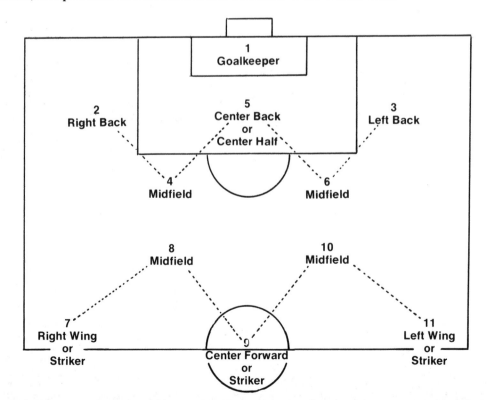

By varying the number of defenders, midfielders, and strikers, formations such as the 4-2-4, the 4-3-3, the 4-4-2, and others have evolved. Some of the modern formations allow one defender to roam either just in front of or just behind the fullbacks. This position is then known as the sweeper, libero, or freeback.

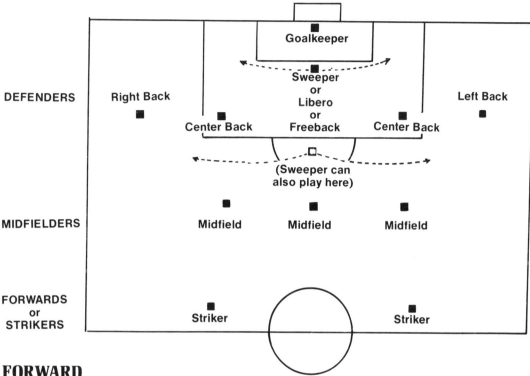

FORWARD

An attacking player on the front line. Also STRIKER.

FOUL

An infraction of the rules of the game. Depending on the gravity of the offense the fouled team is awarded a direct free kick, indirect free kick, or a penalty shot (if the infraction takes place within the penalty area). In the case of a major or repeated infraction, a player may be ejected from the game.

FREEBACK

See SWEEPER.

FREE KICK

A kick awarded by the referee at the location of a foul to the team of the fouled player. No player from the opposing team may be closer than ten yards from the ball until it is kicked. A free kick may be one of two types: (1) Direct—a kick which can be shot directly into the goal, and (2) Indirect—a kick that must touch another player before going into the goal.

FRONT-BLOCK TACKLE

Defender's technique utilizing the legs or body to block or win control of the ball from the front.

FRONT MAN

See TARGET MAN.

FULLBACK

A defender. One of two, three, or four players who plays closest to his own goal. His primary responsibility is to stop the opposing team from attacking the goal area. Also DEFENDER, BACK.

© RAY GOULDSBERRY, 1977

FUNNEL BACK

A defensive strategy in which the defenders fall back in such a way as to encourage attacking opponents to funnel into a sealed-off central area.

GIVE 'N' GO

To pass the ball to a teammate and immediately run toward an open area in order to be in a position to receive a return pass. Also WALL PASS.

GIVING AWAY A CORNER

An expression used when a defender accidentally or deliberately touches the ball just before it crosses the goal line out of play. In such cases the attacking team is awarded a corner kick.

GIVING SOME STICK

Playing rough, physically punishing the opponent.

GOAL

The name for a point scored. (1) When the entire ball crosses the goal line between the goalposts one point is scored. (2) The area bounded by two eight-foot posts twenty-four feet apart and a crossbar that joins them at the top.

GOAL AREA

The small marked rectangle that extends six yards onto the field from a point six yards outside each goalpost. See PITCH.

GOALKEEPER

The last line of defense. The protector of the goal. The only player allowed to use his hands (while he is in the penalty area).

GOAL KICK

An indirect free kick awarded to the defending team when the ball passes over the goal line and is last touched by the attacking team. The kick is taken from inside the goal area on the same side of the goal that the ball went out of bounds. The kick must go out of the penalty area, and the opposing players must stay out of the penalty area until the ball is kicked.

GOAL LINE

The marked boundary line at each end of the playing field between the sidelines or touchlines. See PITCH.

GOALPOSTS

Two eight-foot posts joined at the top by a twenty-four-foot crossbar. The posts mark the sides of the goal.

HALFBACK

See MIDFIELDER.

HALF VOLLEY

A ball that is kicked just as it is rising from a bounce.

HALFWAY LINE

The marked line that crosses the playing field an equal distance from both goal lines. See PITCH.

HANDBALL

An infraction resulting from the intentional touching of the ball with the hands or arms. Also HANDS.

HANDS

See HANDBALL.

HEADER

The act of propelling the ball with the head either toward the goal as a shot, to a teammate as a pass, or out of danger as a clearing pass.

100

HOLDING

The illegal use of hands to obstruct or hold back an opponent.

INDIRECT FREE KICK

A kick awarded after a minor infraction from which a goal cannot be scored directly, but only after it touches another player. No defending player may be closer than ten yards from the ball until the kick is taken.

INDOOR SOCCER

A recent offshoot of traditional soccer played inside an auditorium on a reduced courtlike playing field of artificial turf.

INJURY TIME
Extra time added on by the referee to the end of each half to compensate for time lost during an injury.

INSTEP KICK
A powerful kick utilizing the hard shoelace area of the foot to strike the ball.

INSWINGER
A corner kick in which the ball is kicked in such a way as to make it curve in toward the goal.

INTERFERE

To obstruct the play of an opponent.

IN TO TOUCH

Out of bounds along the touchlines (sidelines). The entire ball must cross the line to be in to touch.

JOCKEYING

See SHEPHERDING.

JUGGLING
The use of the feet, knees, and head to keep the ball controlled and in the air.

KICKOFF

A kick taken from the center spot at the start of each half and after each goal. No opponent may be within ten yards of the ball until the kick is taken. The ball is in play after it has traveled the length of its circumference.

LAWS

The official name for the international rules of soccer. See Part Four for the complete laws of the game.

LIBERO

See SWEEPER.

LINESMAN

A sideline official (two for a game, one on each sideline) whose responsibilities are to watch for and call offside violations and to determine possession (which team takes the throw-in) when the ball crosses a sideline out of play. Linesmen also alert the referee about unseen rule infractions.

© DAVID KEITH 1978

108

LINKMAN

A midfield player between the defense and the offense. Also MIDFIELDER, HALFBACK.

LOFT

To kick the ball in such a way as to lift it into the air. Also FLIGHT.

MAKING SPACE

Drawing opponents away from an area, thereby leaving an undefended space for maneuvering.

MARK

To guard an opponent.

MIDFIELD

The area in the middle of the playing field between the two goals. Most attacks are mounted from this area. It is said that whoever controls the midfield controls the game. See PITCH.

MIDFIELDER

A player whose primary responsibility is to move the ball from the defenders up to the forwards and to control the middle of the field. Midfielders must be able to drop back and help the defense as well as support the attacking forwards. See FORMATIONS.

NARROWING THE ANGLE

Goalkeeper's technique of moving off the goal line toward an advancing opponent who is about to shoot the ball, thereby diminishing the amount of unobstructed goal the opponent has to shoot at.

NASL

The North American Soccer League, the larger of the two soccer leagues in North America. Founded in 1967 when two unsuccessful leagues merged, the NASL is now recognized around the world.

In 1978 the NASL numbered twenty four franchises split into two conferences each comprised three four-team divisions.

AMERICAN CONFERENCE	NATIONAL CONFERENCE
EASTERN DIVISION	
New England Tea Men	Toronto Metro-Croatia
Philadelphia Fury	Rochester Lancers
Tampa Bay Rowdies	New York Cosmos
Ft. Lauderdale Strikers	Washington Diplomats

AMERICAN CONFERENCE	NATIONAL CONFERENCE

CENTRAL DIVISION

Detroit Express		Minnesota Kicks	
Chicago Sting		Atlanta Chiefs	
Memphis Rogues		Tulsa Roughnecks	
Houston Hurricane		Dallas Tornado	

WESTERN DIVISION

Oakland Stompers		Portland Timbers	
San Jose Earthquakes		Seattle Sounders	
California Surf		Vancouver Whitecaps	
San Diego Sockers		Los Angeles Aztecs	

NEAR POST

The goalpost nearer the ball. In corner-kick situations the post nearer the corner from which the kick is taken.

NUTMEG

To get past an opponent by kicking the ball through his legs while moving around him. Defenders consider this to be one of the most humiliating ways of being beaten.

OBSTRUCTION

The blocking of an opponent's path or any attempt to keep an opponent away from the ball.

OFFICIAL TIME

The actual time of the game kept by the referee, who alone controls the stoppage of play and the clock during the soccer match.

OFFSIDE

An infraction that occurs when an attacking player without the ball has less than two defenders between himself and the goal line in the attacking zone (in the NASL within the marked thirty-five-yard offside limit) at the time the ball is played or passed forward by a teammate. A player cannot be offside if: (1) there are two opponents nearer the goal line; (2) he is in his own half of the field; (3) the ball is received directly from a corner kick, goal kick, throw-in or drop ball.

© WILLIE HUNT, 1977

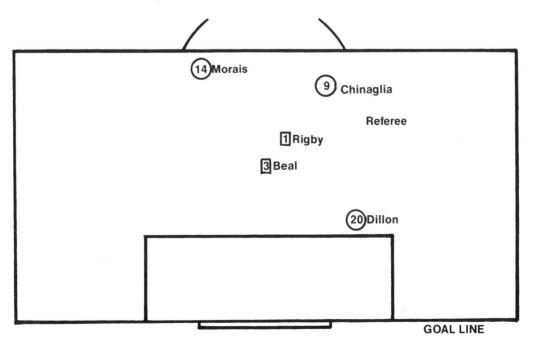

Referee stops play as #20 is offside as shot is taken.

OFFSIDE TRAP

A defensive strategy used most often in free-kick situations whereby the defenders move forward together just before the kick, thus leaving the attackers offside and nullifying the attack.

The offside trap must be used with discretion because of the possibility of the offside infringement going undetected by the referee and linesmen with the constant movement of players.

Defenders X, Y, and Z move forward before attacking player A takes the free kick, trapping B and C offside.

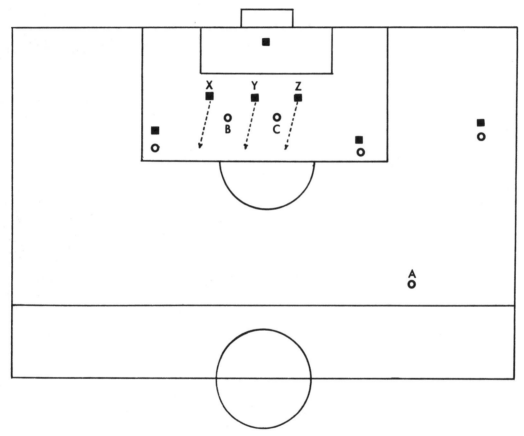

Defender X, Y and Z before attacking player A takes the free kick, trapping B and C offside.

OFF THE BALL RUNNING

Running without the ball in order to seek a better position for a pass, to fool an opponent, or to make space for a teammate.

A goalkeeper's move from the goal line toward an attacking player to narrow the shooting angle and force the opponent to shoot from farther out.

ONE TOUCH

Playing an oncoming ball, whether it is in the air or on the ground, without first trapping or controlling it. See FIRST TIME.

ON THE BALL
In control of the ball. Also DRIBBLING.

ON THE TURN
Turning to face or shoot at the goal while being closely marked.

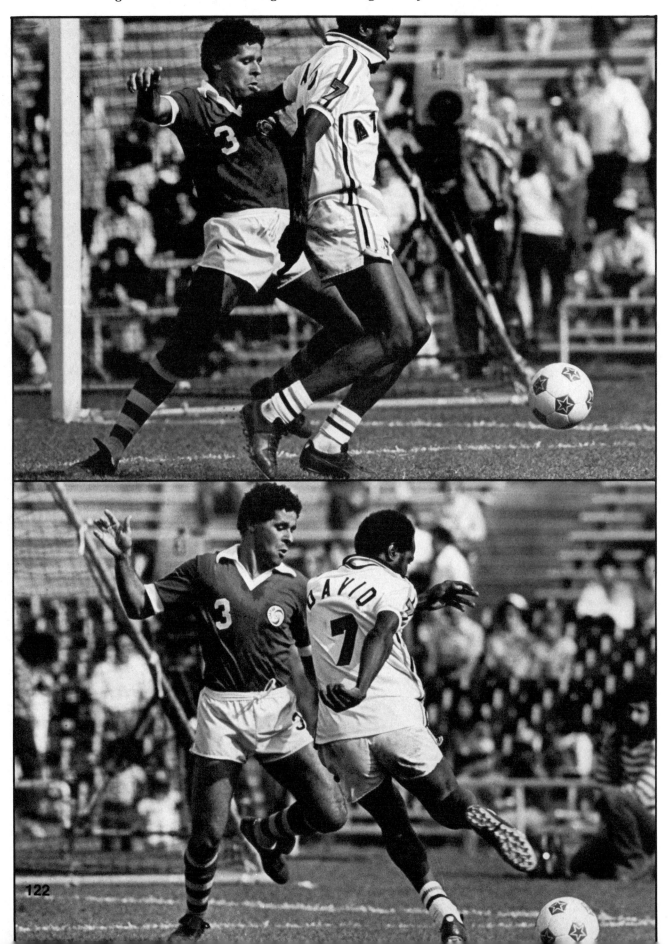

OUTSIDE LEFT

The left winger. The player playing closest to the left sideline. See FORMATIONS.

OUTSIDE RIGHT

The right winger. The player playing closest to the right sideline. See FORMATIONS.

OUTSWINGER

A corner kick in which the ball is kicked in such a way as to curve outward from the goal mouth.

OVERHEAD VOLLEY

A technique whereby a player about to receive a shoulder- or head-high air ball falls backward while thrusting his legs upward in a scissorslike movement to meet the ball and drive it backward over his head. Also BICYCLE KICK.

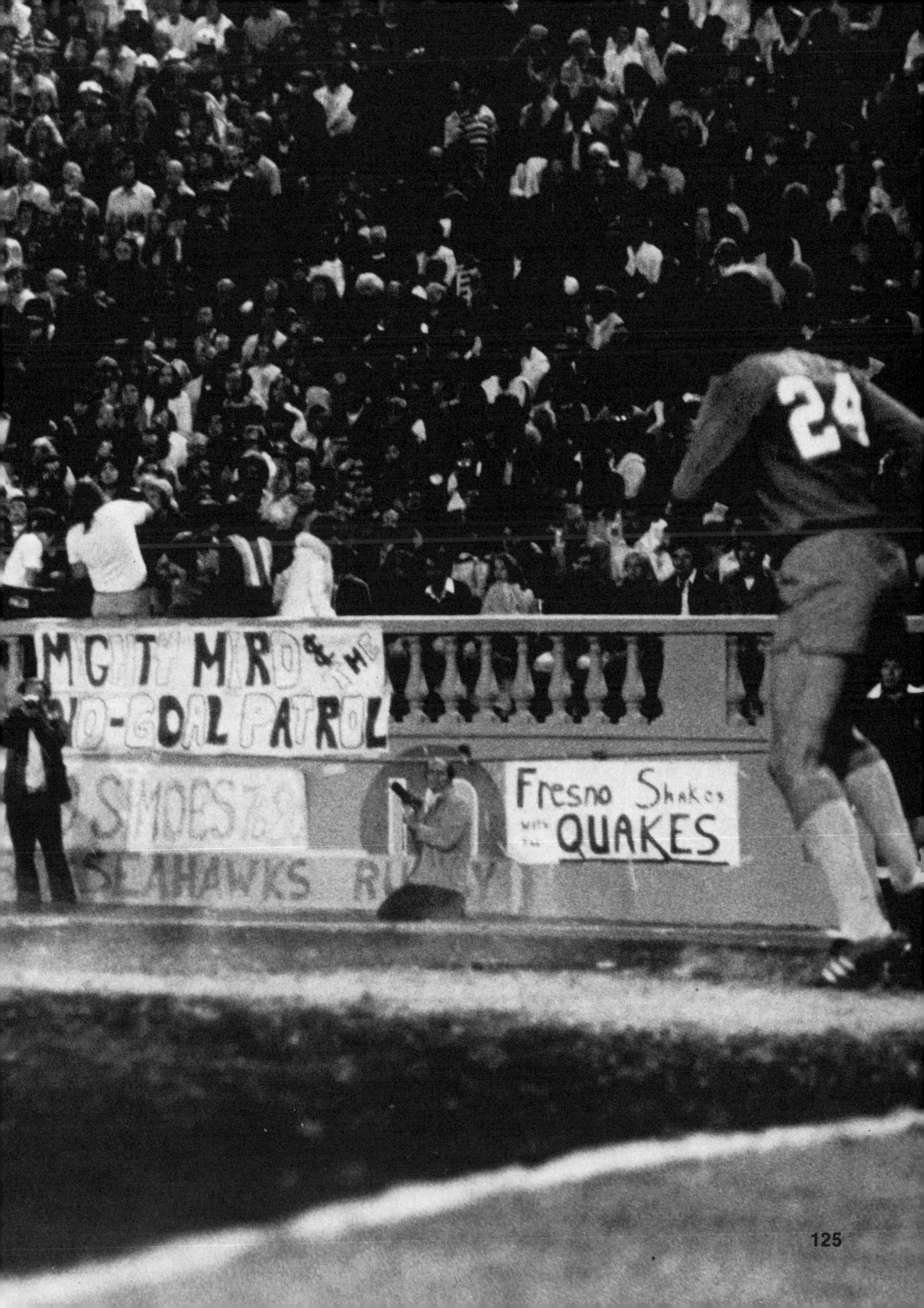
GOAL PATROL
Fresno Shakes
QUAKES
SEAHAWKS
24

OVERLAPPING

A defensive player assuming an attacking role momentarily becoming an extra forward.

OWN GOAL

A goal last touched by a defender.

PACE

The speed with which the game is played or the speed of a moving ball.

PASS

To kick or head the ball toward a teammate.

PENALTY ARC

The arc drawn outside each penalty area with a ten-yard radius from the penalty spot. No player other than the kicker may be inside the penalty arc at the time of a penalty kick. See PITCH.

PENALTY AREA

The forty-four-by-eighteen-yard marked box in front of each goal. If any major foul is committed against an attacking player within this area a penalty shot is awarded to the attacking team. See PITCH.

PENALTY KICK

A direct free kick taken from the penalty spot awarded to the attacking team when a major foul is committed against an attacking player within the marked penalty area. The goalkeeper must stand on the goal line and may not move his feet until the ball is kicked.

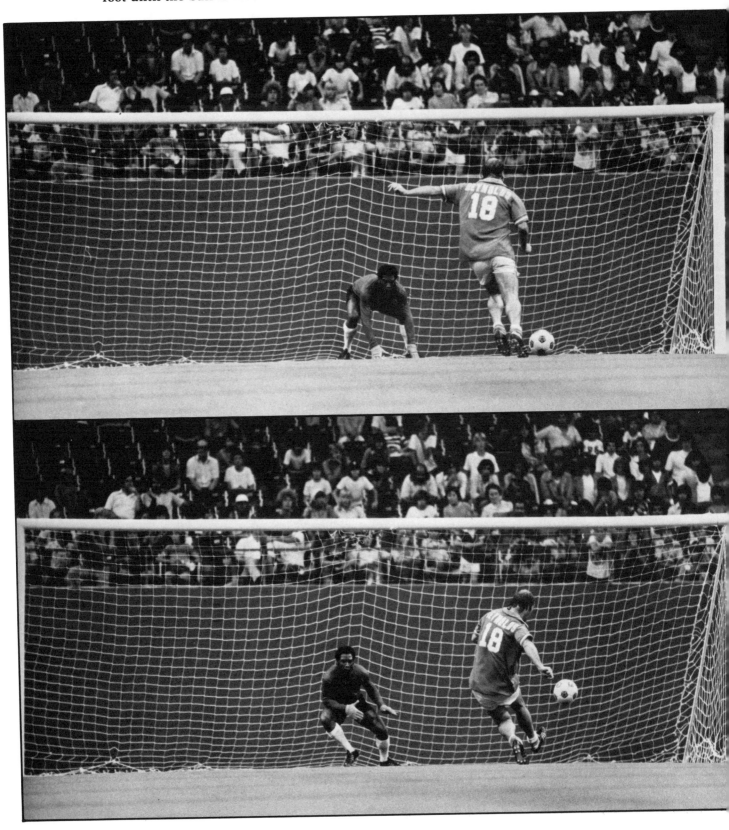

PENALTY SPOT

A spot marked twelve yards out into the penalty area from the middle of the goal. The place where penalty kicks are taken from. See PITCH.

PITCH

The field soccer is played on. See Part Four, Law I.

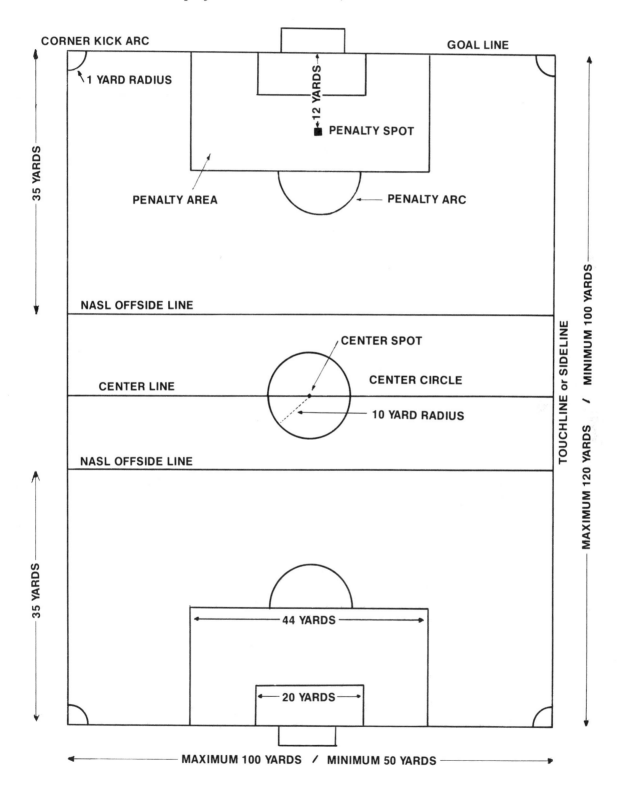

PLAY

To kick or head the ball either as a shot at the goal or as a pass to a teammate.

PULLING THE BALL BACK

A centering pass into the penalty area in front of the goal from a point near the goal line but off to one side of the goal.

PUNCH SAVE

Goalkeeper's technique utilizing a clenched fist or clenched fists to punch an air ball clear of the goal mouth. Also FIST.

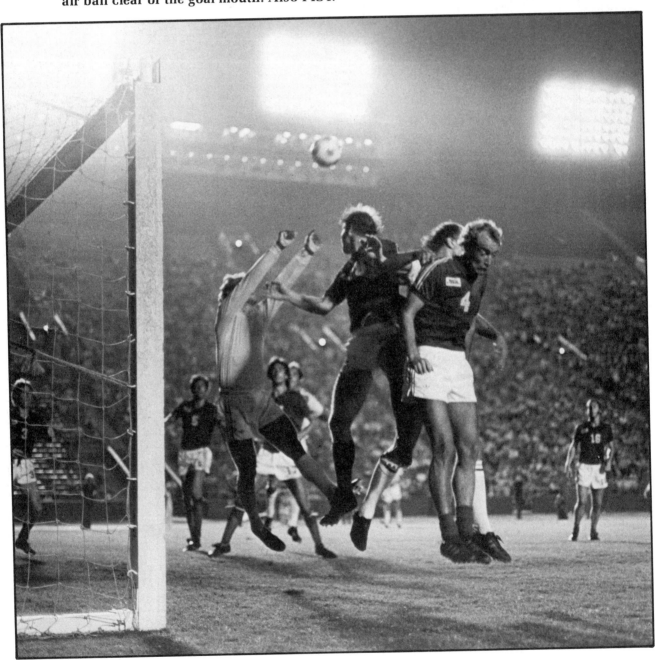

PUNT

The kick used by goalkeepers for distance. The ball is dropped and kicked before it touches the ground.

PUSHING OFF

The use of the hands or arms to push an opponent and gain an advantage; an infraction.

PUSH PASS
A short pass utilizing the inside of the foot to push the ball ahead.

RED CARD

A card shown to an offending player by the referee signifying his ejection from the game for a serious infraction. An ejected player may not be replaced.

REFEREE

The official in charge of a soccer match. The referee keeps the game time, is empowered to stop or terminate the game, call fouls, assess penalties and restart the game after a stoppage of play.

RESTART

The official recommencement of the game after a stoppage of play. A kick off, a dropball, a goal kick, a corner kick and a throw in are examples of a restart.

RIDING A TACKLE
Maintaining control of the ball in spite of a tackle attempt.

SAVE

The art of blocking or stopping the ball from crossing the goal line to score.

SCISSORS VOLLEY

A leaping horizontal kick of an air ball in which the player's legs move like scissors in the act of kicking. When the scissors volley is properly executed it is one of the most spectacular and powerful shots in soccer.

SCREENING

Utilization of the body to protect and shield the ball from an opponent. Legal only when actually playing the ball. Otherwise an interference infraction. Also SHIELDING.

SELLING THE DUMMY

Making an opponent take a specific fake or feint and momentarily commit himself.

SENT OFF

Ejected from the game by the referee. Also EJECTION, RED CARD.

SET-PIECE PLAY

Prearranged team strategy for dead-ball situations with specific assignments for certain players.

SHADOW
To mark or closely guard an opponent throughout a match.

SHEPHERDING

The defensive technique of moving or herding an attacking player out of and away from the goal area. Also JOCKEYING.

SHIELDING

See SCREENING.

SHOOTOUT

The NASL procedure for deciding the outcome of a game that is tied after two seven-minute, thirty-second "sudden death" periods that follow regulation play. Beginning with the visiting team and alternating after each attempt, five players from each side individually challenge the goalkeeper. They start at the thirty-five-yard line, and at a signal from the referee, each player has five seconds to shoot. The goalkeeper has no restrictions on his movement. If the teams remain tied after five attempts each, alternate players continue to shoot until one team scores more times than the other. Only those players who were playing at the end of the overtime period are eligible, and no player may shoot twice until all eligible teammates have made one attempt.

SHOULDER CHARGE

The use of the shoulder and upper part of the arm against the same part of the opponent's body. This is legal if the ball is within playing distance, but an infraction if not or if the charge is judged dangerous by the referee. See CHARGING.

SHOW THE BALL

To tempt a defender to challenge and thereby commit to a course of action by displaying the ball in a seemingly vulnerable position.

SIDE

A team.

SIDE-BLOCK TACKLE

Defensive technique utilizing the foot to block or win control of the ball from the side.

SLIDING TACKLE

A defensive technique where the defender lunges with one foot in order to slide into and dislodge the ball from the opponent.

SPACE

An open unguarded area that can be exploited by the attacking team.

SQUARE PASS

A lateral pass directly to the side.

STEPPING OVER THE BALL

A dribbling trick where a player fakes moving in one direction by shifting his weight as he appears to move the ball the same way with the inside of his foot. He instead steps over the ball and quickly moves it in the opposite direction by flicking the ball with the outside of his foot.

STOPPER

The central defender, lined up opposite, and expected to stop, the opposing striker. Also CENTER BACK, CENTER HALF.

STRIKER

Generally a forward in the center of the front line. The attacking player most often in scoring position. Also CENTER FORWARD. See FORMATIONS.

STRIP

Soccer uniform.

SWEEPER

A roaming defender positioned behind or just in front of the backline to intercept any attacker who breaks through. Also FREEBACK, LIBERO.

TACKLE

A defensive technique utilizing the feet to dislodge or win control of the ball from an opponent.

TARGETMAN
One player, usually a tall striker, who stands alone in an attacking position waiting for a long or centering pass from a teammate. (2) A midfield player, usually tall, who waits for long passes from defending teammates and then distributes the ball to attacking forwards. Also FRONTMAN.

THIG TRAP
Use of the thigh to stop and control an air ball.

THROUGH
Past the last line of defenders.

A pass that goes by the last line of defenders into an open space where a
running attacker can reach the ball before the goalkeeper or defender.

THROW-IN

The method of restarting the game after the ball crosses the sideline. The linesman determines which player last touched the ball, and the other team is awarded the throw-in. The ball must be thrown with both hands over the head, and both feet must be on the ground.

TOUCHLINE

Sideline. See PITCH.

TRAP

To stop and control the ball with the head, chest, body, thigh, or foot.

TRIPPING

An infraction when a player is knocked down by impeding the movement of his legs.

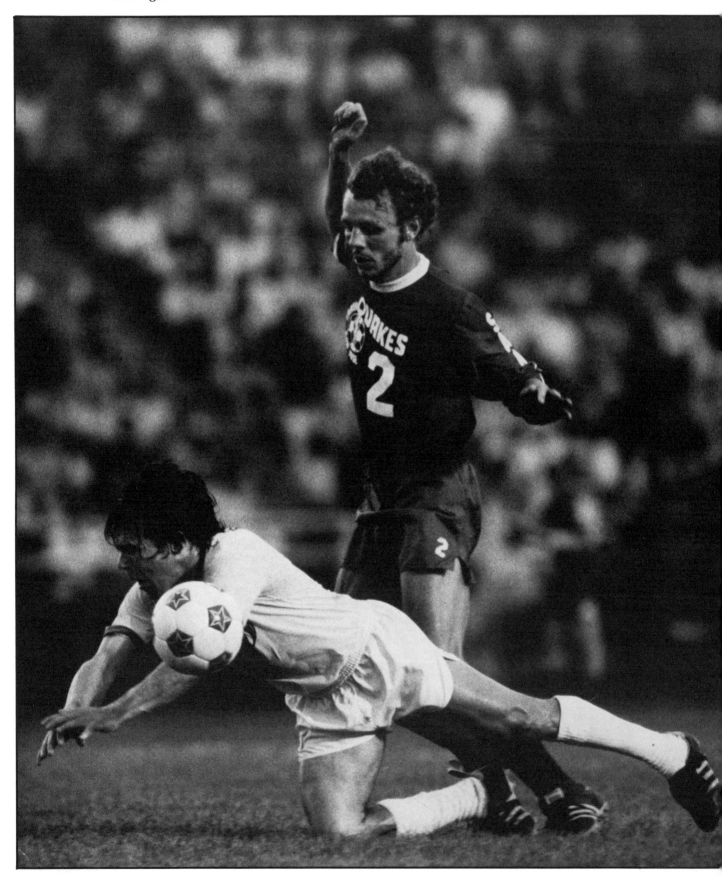

TURNING A DEFENDER

Making a defender turn one way with a fake while actually taking the ball around him the other way.

USSF

The United States Soccer Federation, the governing body for organized soccer in the United States, recognized by FIFA since 1914. USSF is responsible for the selection and training of the U.S. Olympic team, the Pan American team, and the U.S. national team, as well as for directing and encouraging national youth and collegiate soccer programs.

1978 United States Olympic "B" team (under 21).

VOLLEY
A ball kicked while it is in the air.

WALL

A defensive alignment when a free kick is taken from dangerously near the goal. A number of players (depending on the location of the free kick) line up next to each other to form a human wall ten yards from the ball in order to block most of the target area of the goal.

WALL PASS

A technique whereby a player with the ball passes off to a teammate when confronted by a defender and immediately runs past the defender in order to receive a return pass. Also GIVE 'N GO.

WING

The area of the playing field along the sideline.

WINGER

The players positioned along the outside of the forward line. Also OUTSIDE LEFT, OUTSIDE RIGHT.

WINGHALF

The name for players positioned on the outside of the middle line. Also HALFBACK, LINKMAN, MIDFIELDER. See FORMATIONS.

WINNING THE BALL
Taking the ball from the opponent.

WORLD CUP

The premier international competition sanctioned by FIFA. Every four years sixteen national teams that survive elimination playoffs go to the finals. (98 nations took part in eliminations for the 1978 World Cup.) The United States has qualified only three times since the World Cup began in 1930. The last time was in 1950, when the United States shocked the world by defeating England in an early round before being eliminated.

YELLOW CARD

A card shown by the referee to a player guilty of a serious infraction of the rules, and official notice that the player's actions will be reported to the league. Issued for illegal entry or departure from the playing field, continual infractions of the rules, verbal or physical dissent with the referee, or ungentlemanly conduct. Also BOOKING, CAUTION.

Part Three:
The Official Laws of Soccer

LAW I. – THE FIELD OF PLAY

The Field of Play and appurtenances shall be as shown in the following plan:

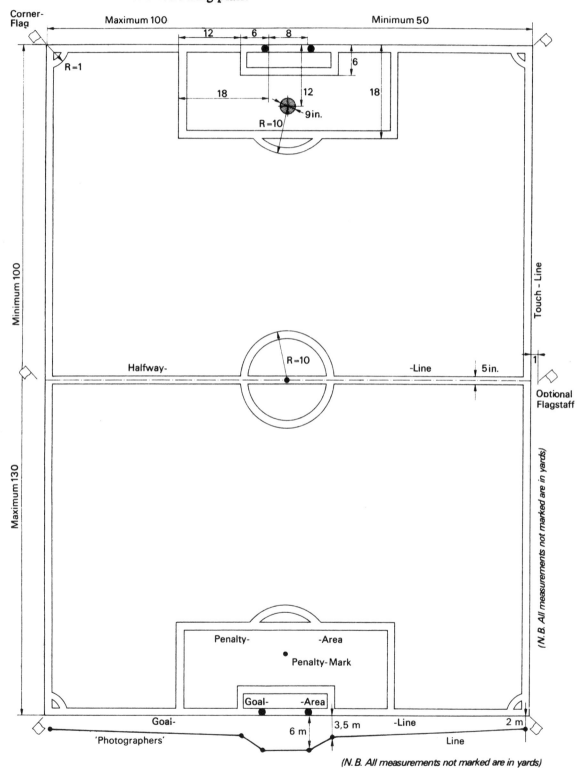

(N.B. All measurements not marked are in yards)

LAW I (continued)

(1) **Dimensions.** The field of play shall be rectangular, its length being not more than 130 yards nor less than 100 yards and its breadth not more than 100 yards nor less than 50 yards. (In International Matches the length shall be not more than 120 yards nor less than 110 yards and the breadth not more than 80 yards nor less than 70 yards.) The length shall in all cases exceed the breadth.

(2) **Marking.** The field of play shall be marked with distinctive lines, not more than 5 inches in width, not by a V-shaped rut, in accordance with the plan, the longer boundary lines being called the touch-lines and the shorter the goal-lines. A flag on a post not less than 5 ft. high and having a non-pointed top, shall be placed at each corner; a similar flag-post may be placed opposite the half-way line on each side of the field of play, not less than 1 yard outside the touch-line. A halfway-line shall be marked out across the field of play. The centre of the field of play shall be indicated by a suitable mark and a circle with a 10 yards radius shall be marked round it.

(3) **The Goal-Area.** At each end of the field of play two lines shall be drawn at right-angles to the goal-line, 6 yards from each goal-post. These shall extend into the field of play for a distance of 6 yards and shall be joined by a line drawn parallel with the goal-line. Each of the spaces enclosed by these lines and the goal-line shall be called a goal-area.

(4) **The Penalty-Area.** At each end of the field of play two lines shall be drawn at right-angles to the goal-line, 18 yards from each goal-post. These shall extend into the field of play for a distance of 18 yards and shall be joined by a line drawn parallel with the goal-line. Each of the spaces enclosed by these lines and the goal-line shall be called a penalty-area. A suitable mark shall be made within each penalty-area, 12 yards from the mid-point of the goal-line, measured along an undrawn line at right-angles thereto. These shall be the penalty-kick marks. From each penalty-kick mark an arc of a circle, having a radius of 10 yards, shall be drawn outside the penalty-area.

(1) In International matches the dimensions of the field of play shall be: maximum 110 x 75 metres; minimum 100 x 64 metres.

(2) National Associations must adhere strictly to these dimensions. Each National Association organising an International Match must advise the visiting Association, before the match, of the place and the dimensions of the field of play.

(3) The Board has approved this table of measurements for the Laws of the Game:

130 yards	. . . . .	120 Metres
120 yards	. . . . .	110
110 yards	. . . . .	100
100 yards	. . . . .	90
80 yards	. . . . .	75
70 yards	. . . . .	64
50 yards	. . . . .	45
18 yards	. . . . .	16.50
12 yards	. . . . .	11
10 yards	. . . . .	9.15
8 yards	. . . . .	7.32
6 yards	. . . . .	5.50
1 yard	. . . . .	1
8 feet	. . . . .	2.44
5 feet	. . . . .	1.50
28 inches	. . . . .	0.71
27 inches	. . . . .	0.68
9 inches	. . . . .	0.22
5 inches	. . . . .	0.12
3/4 inch	. . . . .	0.019
1/2 inch	. . . . .	0.0127
3/8 inch	. . . . .	0.010
14 ounces	. . . . .	396 grams
16 ounces	. . . . .	453 grams
15 lb./sq.in.	. . . . .	1 kg/cm^2

(4) The goal-line shall be marked the same width as the depth of the goal-posts and the cross-bar, so that the goal-line and goal-posts will conform to the same interior and exterior edges.

(5) The 6 yards (for the outline of the goal-area) and the 18 yards (for the outline of the penalty-area) which have to be measured along the goal-line, must start from the inner sides of the goal-posts.

(6) The space within the inside areas of the field of play includes the width of the lines marking these areas.

(7) All Associations shall provide standard equipment, particularly in International Matches, when the Laws of the Game must be complied with in every respect and especially with regard to the size of the ball and other equipment which must conform to the regu-

LAW 1 *(continued)*

(5) **The Corner-Area.** From each corner-flag post a quarter circle, having a radius of 1 yard, shall be drawn inside the field of play.

(6) **The Goals.** The goals shall be placed on the centre of each goal-line and shall consist of two upright posts, equidistant from the corner-flags and 8 yards apart (inside measurement), joined by a horizontal cross-bar the lower edge of which shall be 8 ft. from the ground. The width and depth of the goal-posts and the width and depth of the cross-bars shall not exceed 5 inches (12 cm). The goal-posts and the cross-bars shall have the same width.

Nets may be attached to the posts, cross-bars and ground behind the goals. They should be appropriately supported and be so placed as to allow the goal-keeper ample room.

Footnote:

Goal nets. The use of nets made of hemp, jute or nylon is permitted. The nylon strings may, however, not be thinner than those made of hemp or jute.

lations. All cases of failure to provide standard equipment must be reported to F.I.F.A.

(8) In a match played under the Rules of a Competition if the cross-bar becomes displaced or broken play shall be stopped and the match abandoned unless the cross-bar has been repaired and replaced in position or a new one provided without such being a danger to the players. A rope is not considered to be a satisfactory substitute for a cross-bar.

In a Friendly Match, by mutual consent, play may be resumed without the cross-bar provided it has been removed and no longer constitutes a danger to the players. In these circumstances, a rope may be used as a substitute for a cross-bar. If a rope is not used and the ball crosses the goal-line at a point which in the opinion of the Referee is below where the cross-bar should have been he shall award a goal.

The game shall be restarted by the Referee dropping the ball at the place where it was when play was stopped.

(9) National Associations may specify such maximum and minimum dimensions for the cross-bars and goal-posts, within the limits laid down in Law I, as they consider appropriate.

(10) Goal-posts and cross-bars must be made of wood, metal or other approved material as decided from time to time by the International F.A. Board. They may be square, rectangular, round, half-round or elliptical in shape Goal-posts and cross-bars made of other materials and in other shapes are not permitted.

(11) 'Curtain-raisers' to International matches should only be played following agreement on the day of the match, and taking into account the condition of the field of play, between representatives of the two Associations and the Referee (of the International Match).

(12) National Associations, particularly in International Matches, should
- restrict the number of photographers around the field of play,
- have a line ("photographers' line") marked behind the goal-lines at least two metres from the corner flag going through a point situated at least 3.5 metres behind the intersection of the goal-line with the line marking the goal area to a point

situated at least six metres behind the goal-posts,
- prohibit photographers from passing over these lines,
- forbid the use of artificial lighting in the form of "flashlights".

LAW II. – THE BALL

The ball shall be spherical; the outer casing shall be of leather or other approved materials. No material shall be used in its construction which might prove dangerous to the players.

The circumference of the ball shall not be more than 28 in. and not less than 27 in. The weight of the ball at the start of the game shall not be more than 16 oz. nor less than 14 oz. The pressure shall be equal to 0.6-0.7 atmosphere, which equals 9.0-10.5 lb./sq.in. (= 600-700 gr/cm²) at sea level. The ball shall not be changed during the game unless authorised by the Referee.

(1) The ball used in any match shall be considered the property of the Association or Club on whose ground the match is played, and at the close of play it must be returned to the Referee.

(2) The International Board, from time to time, shall decide what constitutes approved materials. Any approved material shall be certified as such by the International Board.

(3) The Board has approved these equivalents of the weights specified in the Law: 14 to 16 ounces = 396 to 453 grammes.

(4) If the ball bursts or becomes deflated during the course of a match, the game shall be stopped and restarted by dropping the new ball at the place where the first ball became defective.

(5) If this happens during a stoppage of the game (place-kick, goal-kick, corner-kick, free-kick, penalty-kick or throw-in) the game shall be restarted accordingly.

LAW III. – NUMBER OF PLAYERS

(1) A match shall be played by two teams, each consisting of not more than eleven players, one of whom shall be the goalkeeper.

(2) Substitutes may be used in any match played under the rules of an official competition at FIFA, Confederation or National Association level, subject to the following conditions:

(a) that the authority of the international association(s) or national association(s) concerned, has been obtained,

(b) that, subject to the restriction contained in the following paragraph (c) the rules of a competition shall state how many, if any, substitutes may be used, and

(c) that a team shall not be permitted to use more than two substitutes in any match.

(3) Substitutes may be used in any other match, provided that the two teams concerned reach agreement on a maximum number, not exceeding five, and that the terms of such agreement are intimated to the Referee, before the match. If the Referee is not informed, or if the teams fail to reach agreement, no more than two substitutes shall be permitted.

(4) Any of the other players may change places with the goalkeeper, provided that the Referee is informed before the change is made, and provided also, that the change is made during a stoppage in the game.

(5) When a goalkeeper or any other player is to be replaced by a substitute, the following conditions shall be observed:

(a) the Referee shall be informed of the proposed substitution, before it is made,

(b) the substitute shall not enter the field of play until the player he is replacing has left, and then only after having received a signal from the Referee,

(c) he shall enter the field during a stoppage in the game, and at the half-way line.

Punishment:

(a) Play shall not be stopped for an infringement of paragraph 4. The players concerned shall be cautioned immediately the ball goes out of play.

(b) For any other infringement of this law, the player concerned shall be cautioned, and if the game is stopped by the Referee, to administer the caution, it shall be re-started by an indirect free-kick, to be taken by a player of the opposing team, from the place where the ball was, when play was stopped.

(1) The minimum number of players in a team is left to the discretion of National Associations.

(2) The Board is of the opinion that a match should not be considered valid if there are fewer than seven players in either of the teams.

(3) A competition may require that the referee shall be informed, before the start of the match, of the names of not more than five players, from whom the substitutes (if any) must be chosen.

(4) A player who has been ordered off before play begins may only be replaced by one of the named substitutes. The kick-off must not be delayed to allow the substitute to join his team.

A player who has been ordered off after play has started may not be replaced.

A named substitute who has been ordered off, either before or after play has started, may not be replaced (this decision only relates to players who are ordered off under Law XII. It does not apply to players who have infringed Law IV.)

(5) A player who has been replaced shall not take any further part in the game.

(6) A substitute shall be deemed to be a player and shall be subject to the authority and jurisdiction of the Referee whether called upon to play or not. For any offence committed on the field of play a substitute shall be subject to the same punishment as any other player whether called upon or not.

LAW IV. – PLAYERS' EQUIPMENT

(1) A player shall not wear anything which is dangerous to another player.

(2) Footwear (boots or shoes) must conform to the following standard:

(a) Bars shall be made of leather or rubber and shall be transverse and flat, not less than half an inch in width and shall extend the total width of the sole and be rounded at the corners.

(b) Studs which are independently mounted on the sole and are replaceable shall be made of leather, rubber, aluminium, plastic or similar material and shall be solid. With the exception of that part of the stud forming the base, which shall not protrude from the sole more than one quarter of an inch, studs shall be round in plan and not less than half an inch in diameter. Where studs are tapered, the minimum diameter of any section of the stud must not be less than half an inch. Where metal seating for the screw type is used, this seating must be embedded in the sole of the footwear and any atachment screw shall be part of the stud. Other than the metal seating for the screw type of stud, no metal plates even though covered with leather or rubber shall be worn, neither studs which are threaded to allow them to be screwed on to a base screw that is fixed by nails or otherwise to the soles of footwear, nor studs which, apart from the base, have any form of protruding edge rim or relief marking or ornament, should be allowed.

(c) Studs which are moulded as an integral part of the sole and are not replaceable shall be made of rubber, plastic, polyurethene or similar soft materials. Provided that there are no fewer than ten studs on the sole, they shall have a minimum diameter of three eights of an inch (10 mm.). Additional supporting material to stabilise studs of soft materials, and ridges which shall not protrude more than 5 mm. from the sole and moulded to strengthen it, shall be permitted provided that they are in no way dangerous to other players. In all other respects they shall conform to the general requirements of this Law.

(d) Combined bars and studs may be worn, provided the whole conforms to the general requirements of this Law. Neither bars nor studs on the soles shall project more

(1) The usual equipment of a player is a jersey or shirt, shorts, stockings and footwear. In a match played under the rules of a competition, players need not wear boots or shoes, but shall wear jersey or shirt, shorts, or track suit or similar trousers, and stockings.

(2) The Law does not insist that boots or shoes must be worn. However, in competition matches Referees should not allow one or a few players to play without footwear when all the other players are so equipped.

(3) In International Matches, International Competitions, International Club Competitions and friendly matches between clubs of different National Associations, the Referee, prior to the start of the game, shall inspect the players' footwear, and prevent any player whose footwear does not conform to the requirements of this Law from playing until such time as it does comply.

The rules of any competition may include a similar provision.

(4) If the Referee finds that a player is wearing articles not permitted by the Laws and which may constitute a danger to other players, he shall order him to take them off. If he fails to carry out the Referee's instruction, the player shall not take part in the match.

(5) A player who has been prevented from taking part in the game or a player who has been sent off the field for infringing Law IV must report to the Referee during a stoppage of the game and may not enter or re-enter the field of play unless and until the Referee has satisfied himself that the player is no longer infringing Law IV.

(6) A player who has been prevented from taking part in a game or who has been sent off because of an infringement of Law IV, and who enters or re-enters the field of play to join or re-join his team, in breach of the conditions of Law XII, shall be cautioned. If the Referee stops the game to administer the caution, the game shall be restarted by an indirect free-kick, taken by a player of the opposing side, from the place where the ball was when the Referee stopped the game.

LAW IV *(continued)*

than three-quarters of an inch. If nails are used they shall be driven in flush with the surface.

(3) The goalkeeper shall wear colours which distinguish him from the other players and from the referee.

Punishment: For any infringement of this Law, the player at fault shall be sent off the field of play to adjust his equipment and he shall not return without first reporting to the Referee, who shall satisfy himself that the player's equipment is in order; the player shall only re-enter the game at a moment when the ball has ceased to be in play.

LAW V. – REFEREES

A Referee shall be appointed to officiate in each game. His authority and the exercise of the powers granted to him by the Laws of the Game commence as soon as he enters the field of play.

His power of penalising shall extend to offences committed when play has been temporarily suspended, or when the ball is out of play. His decision on points of fact connected with the play shall be final, so far as the result of the game is concerned. He shall:

(a) Enforce the Laws.

(b) Refrain from penalising in cases where he is satisfied that, by doing so, he would be giving an advantage to the offending team.

(c) Keep a record of the game; act as timekeeper and allow the full or agreed time, adding thereto all time lost through accident or other cause.

(d) Have discretionary power to stop the game for any infringement of the Laws and to suspend or terminate the game whenever, by reason of the elements, interference by spectators, or other cause, he deems such stoppage necessary. In such a case he shall submit a detailed report to the competent authority, within the stipulated time, and in accordance with the provisions set up by the National Association under whose jurisdiction the match was played. Reports will be deemed to be made when received in the ordinary course of post.

(e) From the time he enters the field of play, caution any player guilty of misconduct or ungentlemanly behaviour and, if he persists, suspend him from further participation in the game. In such cases the Referee shall send the name of the offender to the competent authority, within the stipulated time, and in accordance with the provisions set up by the National Association under whose jurisdiction the match was played. Reports will be deemed to be made when received in the ordinary course of post.

(f) Allow no person other than the players and linesmen to enter the field of play without his permission.

(g) Stop the game if, in his opinion, a player has been seriously injured; have the player removed as soon as possible from the

(1) Referees in International Matches shall wear a blazer or blouse the colour of which is distinct from the colours worn by the contesting teams.

(2) Referees for International Matches will be selected from a neutral country unless the countries concerned agree to appoint their own officials.

(3) The Referee must be chosen from the official list of International Referees. This need not apply to Amateur and Youth International Matches.

(4) The Referee shall report to the appropriate authority misconduct or any misdemeanour on the part of spectators, officials, players, named substitutes or other persons which take place either on the field of play or in its vicinity at any time prior to, during, or after the match in question so that appropriate action can be taken by the Authority concerned.

(5) Linesmen are assistants of the Referee. In no case shall the Referee consider the intervention of a Linesman if he himself has seen the incident and from his position on the field, is better able to judge. With this reserve, and the Linesman neutral, the Referee can consider the intervention and if the information of the Linesman applies to that phase of the game immediately before the scoring of a goal, the Referee may act thereon and cancel the goal.

(6) The Referee, however, can only reverse his first decision so long as the game has not been restarted.

(7) If the Referee has decided to apply the advantage clause and to let the game proceed, he cannot revoke his decision if the presumed advantage has not been realised, even though he has not, by any gesture, indicated his decision. This does not exempt the offending player from being dealt with by the Referee.

(8) The Laws of the Game are intended to provide that games should be played with as little interference as possible, and in this view it is the duty of Referees to penalise only deliberate breaches of the Law. Constant whistling for trifling and doubtful breaches produces bad feeling and loss of temper on the part of the players and spoils the pleasure of spectators.

(9) By para. (d) of Law V the Referee is

LAW V *(continued)*

field of play, and immediately resume the game. If a player is slightly injured, the game shall not be stopped until the ball has ceased to be in play. A player who is able to go to the touch or goal-line for attention of any kind, shall not be treated on the field of play.

(h) Send off the field of play, any player who, in his opinion, is guilty of violent conduct, serious foul play, or the use of foul or abusive language.

(i) Signal for recommencement of the game after all stoppages.

(j) Decide that the ball provided for a match meets with the requirements of Law II.

empowered to terminate a match in the event of grave disorder, but he has no power or right to decide, in such event, that either team is disqualified and thereby the loser of the match. He must send a detailed report to the proper authority who alone has power to deal further with this matter.

(10) If a player commits two infringements of a different nature at the same time, the Referee shall punish the more serious offence.

(11) It is the duty of the Referee to act upon the information of neutral Linesmen with regard to incidents that do not come under the personal notice of the Referee.

(12) The Referee shall not allow any person to enter the field until play has stopped, and only then, if he has given him a signal to do so, nor shall he allow coaching from the boundary lines.

LAW VI. – LINESMEN

Two Linesmen shall be appointed, whose duty (subject to the decision of the Referee) shall be to indicate when the ball is out of play and which side is entitled to the corner-kick, goal-kick or throw-in. They shall also assist the Referee to control the game in accordance with the Laws. In the event of undue interference or improper conduct by a Linesman, the Referee shall dispense with his services and arrange for a substitute to be appointed. (The matter shall be reported by the Referee to the competent authority.) The Linesmen should be equipped with flags by the Club on whose ground the match is played.

(1) Linesmen, where neutral, shall draw the Referee's attention to any breach of the Laws of the Game of which they become aware if they consider that the Referee may not have seen it, but the Referee shall always be the judge of the decision to be taken.

(2) National Associations are advised to appoint official Referees of neutral nationality to act as Linesmen in International Matches.

(3) In International Matches Linesmen's flags shall be of a vivid colour, bright reds and yellows. Such flags are recommended for use in all other matches.

(4) A Linesman may be subject to disciplinary action only upon a report of the Referee for unjustified interference or insufficient assistance.

LAW VII. – DURATION OF THE GAME

The duration of the game shall be two equal periods of 45 minutes, unless otherwise mutually agreed upon, subject to the following: (a) Allowance shall be made in either period for all time lost through accident or other cause, the amount of which shall be a matter for the discretion of the Referee; (b) Time shall be extended to permit a penalty-kick being taken at or after the expiration of the normal period in either half.

At half-time the interval shall not exceed five minutes except by consent of the Referee.

(1) If a match has been stopped by the Referee, before the completion of the time specified in the rules, for any reason stated in Law V it must be replayed in full unless the rules of the competition concerned provide for the result of the match at the time of such stoppage to stand.

(2) Players have a right to an interval at half-time.

LAW VIII. – THE START OF PLAY

(a) **At the beginning of the game,** choice of ends and the kick-off shall be decided by the toss of a coin. The team winning the toss shall have the option of choice of ends or the kick-off. The Referee having given a signal, the game shall be started by a player taking a place-kick (i.e., a kick at the ball while it is stationary on the ground in the centre of the field of play) into his opponents' half of the field of play. Every player shall be in his own half of the field and every player of the team opposing that of the kicker shall remain not less than 10 yards from the ball until it is kicked-off; it shall not be deemed in play until it has travelled the distance of its own circumference. The kicker shall not play the ball a second time until it has been touched or played by another player.

(b) **After a goal has scored,** the game shall be restarted in like manner by a player of the team losing the goal.

(c) **After half-time;** when restarting after half-time, ends shall be changed and the kick-off shall be taken by a player of the opposite team to that of the player who started the game.

Punishment. For any infringement of this Law, the kick-off shall be retaken, except in the case of the kicker playing the ball again before it has been touched or played by another player; for this offence, an indirect free-kick shall be taken by a player of the opposing team from the place where the infringement occurred. A goal shall not be scored direct from a kick-off.

(d) **After any other temporary suspension;** when restarting the game after a temporary suspension of play from any cause not mentioned elsewhere in these Laws, provided that immediately prior to the suspension the ball has not passed over the touch or goal-lines, the Referee shall drop the ball at the place where it was when play was suspended and it shall be deemed in play when it has touched the ground; if, however, it goes over the touch or goal-lines after it has been dropped by the Referee, but before it is touched by a player, the Referee shall again drop it. A player shall not play the ball until it has touched the ground. If this section of the Law is not complied with the Referee shall again drop the ball.

(1) If, when the Referee drops the ball, a player infringes any of the Laws before the ball has touched the ground, the player concerned shall be cautioned or sent off the field according to the seriousness of the offence, but a free-kick cannot be awarded to the opposing team because the ball was not in play at the time of the offence. The ball shall therefore be again dropped by the Referee.

(2) Kicking-off by persons other than the players competing in a match is prohibited.

LAW IX. – BALL IN AND OUT OF PLAY

The ball is out of play:

(a) When it has wholly crossed the goal-line or touch-line, whether on the ground or in the air.

(b) When the game has been stopped by the Referee.

The ball is in play at all other times from the start of the match to the finish including:

(a) If it rebounds from a goal-post, cross-bar or corner-flag post into the field of play.

(b) If it rebounds off either the Referee or Linesmen when they are in the field of play.

(c) In the event of a supposed infringement of the Laws, until a decision is given.

(1) The lines belong to the areas of which they are the boundaries. In consequence, the touch-lines and the goal-lines belong to the field of play.

LAW X. – METHOD OF SCORING

Except as otherwise provided by these Laws, a goal is scored when the whole of the ball has passed over the goal-line, between the goal-posts and under the cross-bar, provided it has not been thrown, carried or intentionally propelled by hand or arm, by a player of the attacking side, except in the case of a goalkeeper, who is within his own penalty-area.

The team scoring the greater number of goals during a game shall be the winner; if no goals, or an equal number of goals are scored, the game shall be termed a "draw".

(1) Law X defines the only method according to which a match is won or drawn; no variation whatsoever can be authorised.

(2) A goal cannot in any case be allowed if the ball has been prevented by some outside agent from passing over the goal-line. If this happens in the normal course of play, other than at the taking of a penalty-kick: the game must be stopped and restarted by the Referee dropping the ball at the place where the ball came into contact with the interference.

(3) If, when the ball is going into goal, a spectator enters the field before it passes wholly over the goal-line, and tries to prevent a score, a goal shall be allowed if the ball goes into goal unless the spectator has made contact with the ball or has interfered with play, in which case the Referee shall stop the game and restart it by dropping the ball at the place where the contact or interference occurred.

LAW XI. – OFF-SIDE

A player is off-side if he is nearer his opponents' goal-line than the ball **at the moment the ball is played unless:**

(a) He is in his own half of the field of play.

(b) There are two of his opponents nearer to their own goal-line than he is.

(c) The ball last touched an opponent or was last played by him.

(d) He receives the ball direct from a goal-kick, a corner-kick, a throw-in, or when it was dropped by the Referee.

Punishment. For an infringement of this Law, an indirect free-kick shall be taken by a player of the opposing team from the place where the infringement occurred.

A player in an off-side position shall not be penalised unless, in the opinion of the Referee, he is interfering with the play or with an opponent, or is seeking to gain an advantage by being in an offside position.

(1) Off-side shall not be judged at the moment the player in question receives the ball, but at the moment when the ball is passed to him by one of his own side. A player who is not in an off-side position when one of his colleagues passes the ball to him or takes a free-kick, does not therefore become off-side if he goes forward during the flight of the ball.

LAW XII. – FOULS AND MISCONDUCT

A player who intentionally commits any of the following nine offences:

(a) Kicks or attempts to kick an opponent;

(b) Trips an opponent, i.e., throwing or attempting to throw him by the use of the legs or by stooping in front of or behind him;

(c) Jumps at an opponent;

(d) Charges an opponent in a violent or dangerous manner;

(e) Charges an opponent from behind unless the latter be obstructing;

(f) Strikes or attempts to strike an opponent;

(g) Holds an opponent;

(h) Pushes an opponent;

(i) Handles the ball, i.e., carries, strikes or propels the ball with his hand or arm. (This does not apply to the goalkeeper within his own penalty-area);

shall be penalised by the award of a **direct free-kick** to be taken by the opposing side from the place where the offence occurred.

Should a player of the defending side intentionally commit one of the above nine offences within the penalty-area he shall be penalised by a **penalty-kick.**

A penalty-kick can be awarded irrespective of the position of the ball, if in play, at the time an offence within the penalty-area is committed.

A player committing any of the five following offences:

1. Playing in a manner considered by the Referee to be dangerous, e.g., attempting to kick the ball while held by the goalkeeper;

2. Charging fairly, i.e., with the shoulder, when the ball is not within playing distance of the players concerned and they are definitely not trying to play it;

3. When not playing the ball, intentionally obstructing an opponent, i.e., running between the opponent and the ball, or interposing the body so as to form an obstacle to an opponent;

4. Charging the goalkeeper except when he

    (a) is holding the ball;

    (b) is obstructing an opponent;

(1) If the goalkeeper either intentionally strikes an opponent by throwing the ball vigorously at him or pushes him with the ball while holding it, the Referee shall award a penalty-kick, if the offence took place within the penalty-area.

(2) If a player deliberately turns his back to an opponent when he is about to be tackled, he may be charged but not in a dangerous manner.

(3) In case of body-contact in the goal-area between an attacking player and the opposing goalkeeper not in possession of the ball, the Referee, as sole judge of intention, shall stop the game if, in his opinion, the action of the attacking player was intentional, and award an indirect free-kick.

(4) If a player leans on the shoulders of another player of his own team in order to head the ball, the Referee shall stop the game, caution the player for ungentlemanly conduct and award an indirect free-kick to the opposing side.

(5) A player's obligation when joining or rejoining his team after the start of the match to 'report to the Referee' must be interpreted as meaning 'to draw the attention of the Referee from the touch-line'. The signal from the Referee shall be made by a definite gesture which makes the player understand the he may come into the field of play; it is not necessary for the Referee to wait until the game is stopped (this does not apply in respect of an infringement of Law IV), but the Referee is the sole judge of the moment in which he gives his signal of acknowledgement.

(6) The letter and spirit of Law XII do not oblige the Referee to stop a game to administer a caution. He may, if he chooses, apply the advantage. If he does apply the advantage, he shall caution the player when play stops.

(7) If a player covers up the ball without touching it in an endeavour not to have it played by an opponent, he obstructs but does not infringe Law XII para. 3 because he is already in possession of the ball and covers it for tactical reasons whilst the ball remains within playing distance. In fact, he is actually playing the ball and does not commit an infringement; in this case, the

LAW XII *(continued)*
(c) has passed outside his goal-area;

5. When playing as goalkeeper,
    (a) takes more than 4 steps whilst holding, bouncing or throwing the ball in the air and catching it again without releasing it so that it is played by another player, or
    (b) indulges in tactics which, in the opinion of the Referee, are designed merely to hold up the game and thus waste time and so give an unfair advantage to his own team

shall be penalised by the award of an **indirect free-kick** to be taken by the opposing side from the place where the infringement occurred.

A player shall be **cautioned** if:

(j) he enters or re-enters the field of play to join or rejoin his team after the game has commenced, or leaves the field of play during the progress of the game (except through accident) without, in either case, first having received a signal from the Referee showing him that he may do so. If the Referee stops the game to administer the caution the game shall be restarted by an indirect free-kick taken by a player of the opposing team from the place where the ball was when the referee stopped the game. If, however, the offending player has committed a more serious offence he shall be penalised according to that section of the law he infringed;

(k) he persistently infringes the Laws of the Game;

(l) he shows by word or action, dissent from any decision given by the Referee;

(m) he is guilty of ungentlemanly conduct.

For any of these last three offences, in addition to the caution, an **indirect free-kick** shall also be awarded to the opposing side from the place where the offence occurred unless a more serious infringement of the Laws of the Game was committed.

A player shall be **sent off** the field of play, if:

(n) in the opinion of the Referee he is guilty of violent conduct or serious foul play;

(o) he uses foul or abusive language

(p) he persists in misconduct after having received a caution.

player may be charged because he is in fact playing the ball.

(8) If a player intentionally stretches his arms to obstruct an opponent and steps from one side to the other, moving his arms up and down to delay his opponent, forcing him to change course, but does not make "bodily contact" the Referee shall caution the player for ungentlemanly conduct and award an indirect free-kick.

(9) If a player intentionally obstructs the opposing goalkeeper, in an attempt to prevent him from putting the ball into play in accordance with Law XII, 5(a), the referee shall award an indirect free-kick.

(10) If after a Referee has awarded a free-kick a player protests violently by using abusive or foul language and is sent off the field, the free-kick should not be taken until the player has left the field.

(11) Any player, whether he is within or outside the field of play, whose conduct is ungentlemanly or violent, whether or not it is directed towards an opponent, a colleague, the Referee, a linesman or other person, or who uses foul or abusive language, is guilty of an offence, and shall be dealt with according to the nature of the offence committed.

(12) If, in the opinion of the Referee a goalkeeper intentionally lies on the ball longer than is necessary, he shall be penalised for ungentlemanly conduct and
(a) be cautioned and an indirect free-kick awarded to the opposing team;
(b) in case of repetition of the offence, be sent off the field.

(13) The offence of spitting at opponents, officials or other persons, or similar unseemly behaviour shall be considered as violent conduct within the meaning of section (n) of Law XII.

(14) If, when a Referee is about to caution a player, and before he has done so, the player commits another offence which merits a caution, the player shall be sent off the field of play.

LAW XII *(continued)*

If play be stopped by reason of a player being ordered from the field for an offence without a separate breach of the Law having been committed, the game shall be resumed by an **indirect free-kick** awarded to the opposing side from the place where the infringement occurred.

LAW XIII. – FREE-KICK

Free-kicks shall be classified under two headings: "Direct" (from which a goal can be scored direct against the offending side), and "Indirect" (from which a goal cannot be scored unless the ball has been played or touched by a player other than the kicker before passing through the goal).

When a player is taking a direct or an indirect free-kick inside his own penalty-area, all of the opposing players shall remain outside the area, and shall be at least ten yards from the ball whilst the kick is being taken. The ball shall be in play immediately it has travelled the distance of its own circumference and is beyond the penalty-area. The goalkeeper shall not receive the ball into his hands, in order that he may thereafter kick it into play. If the ball is not kicked direct into play, beyond the penalty-area, the kick shall be retaken.

When a player is taking a direct or an indirect free-kick outside his own penalty-area, all of the opposing players shall be at least ten yards from the ball, until it is in play, unless they are standing on their own goal-line, between the goal-posts. The ball shall be in play when it has travelled the distance of its own circumference.

If a player of the opposing side encroaches into the penalty-area, or within ten yards of the ball, as the case may be, before a free-kick is taken, the Referee shall delay the taking of the kick, until the Law is complied with.

The ball must be stationary when a free-kick is taken, and the kicker shall not play the ball a second time, until it has been touched or played by another player.

Punishment. If the kicker, after taking the free-kick, plays the ball a second time before it has been touched or played by another player an indirect free-kick shall be taken by a player of the opposing team from the spot where the infringement occurred.

(1) In order to distinguish between a direct and an indirect free-kick, the Referee, when he awards an indirect free-kick, shall indicate accordingly by raising an arm above his head. He shall keep his arm in that position until the kick has been taken.

(2) Players who do not retire to the proper distance when a free-kick is taken must be cautioned and on any repetition be ordered off. It is particularly requested of Referees that attempts to delay the taking of a free-kick by encroaching should be treated as serious misconduct.

(3) If, when a free-kick is being taken, any of the players dance about or gesticulate in a way calculated to distract their opponents, it shall be deemed ungentlemanly conduct for which the offender(s) shall be cautioned.

LAW XIV. – PENALTY-KICK

A penalty-kick shall be taken from the penalty-mark and, when it is being taken, all players with the exception of the player taking the kick, and the opposing goal-keeper, shall be within the field of play but outside the penalty-area, and at least 10 yards from the penalty-mark. The opposing goalkeeper must stand (without moving his feet) on his own goal-line, between the goal-posts, until the ball is kicked. The player taking the kick must kick the ball forward; he shall not play the ball a second time until it has been touched or played by another player. The ball shall be deemed in play directly it is kicked, i.e., when it has travelled the distance of its circumference, and a goal may be scored direct from such a penalty-kick. If the ball touches the goalkeeper before passing between the posts, when a penalty-kick is being taken at or after the expiration of half-time or full-time, it does not nullify a goal. If necessary, time of play shall be extended at half-time or full-time to allow a penalty-kick to be taken.

Punishment:

For any infringement of this Law:

(a) by the defending team, the kick shall be retaken if a goal has not resulted.

(b) by the attacking team other than by the player taking the kick, if a goal is scored it shall be disallowed and the kick re-taken.

(c) by the player taking the penalty-kick, committed after the ball is in play, a player of the opposing team shall take an indirect free-kick from the spot where the infringement occurred.

(1) When the Referee has awarded a penalty-kick, he shall not signal for it to be taken, until the players have taken up position in accordance with the Law.

(2) (a) If, after the kick has been taken, the ball is stopped in its course towards goal, by an outside agent, the kick shall be retaken.

(b) If, after the kick has been taken, the ball rebounds into play, from the goalkeeper, the cross-bar or a goal-post, and is then stopped in its course by an outside agent, the Referee shall stop play and restart it by dropping the ball at the place where it came into contact with the outside agent.

(3) (a) If, after having given the signal for a penalty-kick to be taken, the Referee sees that the goalkeeper is not in his right place on the goal-line, he shall, nevertheless, allow the kick to proceed. It shall be retaken, if a goal is not scored.

(b) If, after the Referee has given the signal for a penalty-kick to be taken, and before the ball has been kicked, the goalkeeper moves his feet, the Referee shall, nevertheless, allow the kick to proceed. It shall be retaken, if a goal is not scored.

(c) If, after the Referee has given the signal for a penalty-kick to be taken, and before the ball is in play, a player of the defending team encroaches into the penalty-area, or within ten yards of the penalty-mark, the Referee shall, nevertheless, allow the kick to proceed. It shall be retaken, if a goal is not scored.

The player concerned shall be cautioned.

(4) (a) If, when a penalty-kick is being taken, the player taking the kick is guilty of ungentlemanly conduct, the kick, if already taken, shall be retaken, if a goal is scored.

The player concerned shall be cautioned.

(b) If, after the referee has given the signal for a penalty-kick to be taken, and before the ball is in play, a colleague of the player taking the kick encroaches into the penalty-area or within ten yards of the penalty-mark, the Referee shall, nevertheless, allow the kick to proceed. If a goal is scored, it shall be disallowed, and the kick retaken.

The player concerned shall be cautioned.

(c) If, in the circumstances described in the foregoing paragraph, the ball rebounds into play from the goalkeeper, the cross-bar or a goal-post, the Referee shall stop the game, caution the player and award an indirect free-kick to the opposing team from the place where the infringement occurred.

(5) (a) If, after the referee has given the signal for a penalty-kick to be taken, and before the ball is in play, the goalkeeper moves from his position on the goal-line, or moves his feet, and a colleague of the kicker encroaches into the penalty-area or within 10 yards of the penalty-mark, the kick, if taken, shall be retaken.

The colleague of the kicker shall be cautioned.

(b) If, after the Referee has given the signal for a penalty-kick to be taken, and before the ball is in play, a player of each team encroaches into the penalty-area, or within 10 yards of the penalty-mark, the kick, if taken, shall be retaken.

The players concerned shall be cautioned.

(6) When a match is extended, at half-time or full-time, to allow a penalty-kick to be taken or retaken, the extension shall last until the moment that the penalty-kick has been completed, i.e. until the Referee has decided whether or not a goal is scored.

A goal is scored when the ball passes wholly over the goal-line.

(a) direct from the penalty-kick,

(b) having rebounded from either goal-post or the cross-bar, or

(c) having touched or been played by the goalkeeper.

The game shall terminate immediately the Referee has made his decision.

(7) When a penalty-kick is being taken in extended time:

(a) the provisions of all of the foregoing paragraphs, except paragraphs (2) (b) and (4) (c) shall apply in the usual way, and

(b) in the circumstances described in paragraphs (2) (b) and (4) (c) the game shall terminate immediately the ball rebounds from the goalkeeper, the cross-bar or the goal-post.

LAW XV. – THROW-IN

When the whole of the ball passes over a touch-line, either on the ground or in the air, it shall be thrown in from the point where it crossed the line, in any direction, by a player of the team opposite to that of the player who last touched it. The thrower at the moment of delivering the ball must face the field of play and part of each foot shall be either on the touch-line or on the ground outside the touch-line. The thrower shall use both hands and shall deliver the ball from behind and over his head. The ball shall be in play immediately it enters the field of play, but the thrower shall not again play the ball until it has been touched or played by another player. A goal shall not be scored direct from a throw-in.

Punishment:

(a) If the ball is improperly thrown in the throw-in shall be taken by a player of the opposing team.

(b) If the thrower plays the ball a second time before it has been touched or played by another player, an indirect free-kick shall be taken by a player of the opposing team from the place where the infringement occurred.

(1) If a player taking a throw-in, plays the ball a second time by handling it within the field of play before it has been touched or played by another player, the Referee shall award a direct free-kick.

(2) A player taking a throw-in must face the field of play with some part of his body.

(3) If, when a throw-in is being taken, any of the opposing players dance about or gesticulate in a way calculated to distract or impede the thrower, it shall be deemed ungentlemanly conduct, for which the offender(s) shall be cautioned.

LAW XVI. – GOAL-KICK

When the whole of the ball passes over the goal-line excluding that portion between the goal-posts, either in the air or on the ground, having last been played by one of the attacking team, it shall be kicked direct into play beyond the penalty-area from a point within that half of the goal-area nearest to where it crossed the line, by a player of the defending team. A goalkeeper shall not receive the ball into his hands from a goal-kick in order that he may thereafter kick it into play. If the ball is not kicked beyond the penalty-area, i.e., direct into play, the kick shall be retaken. The kicker shall not play the ball a second time until it has touched – or been played by – another player. A goal shall not be scored direct from such a kick. Players of the team opposing that of the player taking the goal-kick shall remain outside the penalty-area whilst the kick is being taken.

Punishment: If a player taking a goal-kick plays the ball a second time after it has passed beyond the penalty-area, but before it has touched or been played by another player, an indirect free-kick shall be awarded to the opposing team, to be taken from the place where the infringement occurred.

(1) When a goal-kick has been taken and the player who has kicked the ball touches it again before it has left the penalty-area, the kick has not been taken in accordance with the Law and must be retaken.

LAW XVII. – CORNER-KICK

When the whole of the ball passes over the goal-line, excluding that portion between the goal-posts, either in the air or on the ground, having last been played by one of the defending team, a member of the attacking team shall take a corner-kick, i.e., the whole of the ball shall be placed within the quarter circle at the nearest corner-flag-post, which must not be moved, and it shall be kicked from that position. A goal may be scored direct from such a kick. Players of the team opposing that of the player taking the corner-kick shall not approach within 10 yards of the ball until it is in play, i.e., it has travelled the distance of its own circumference, nor shall the kicker play the ball a second time until it has been touched or played by another player.

Punishment:

(a) If the player who takes the kick plays the ball a second time before it has been touched or played by another player, the Referee shall award an indirect free-kick to the opposing team, to be taken from the place where the infringement occurred.

(b) For any other infringement the kick shall be retaken.

Part Four:
Index of Photographs and Milestones in American Soccer

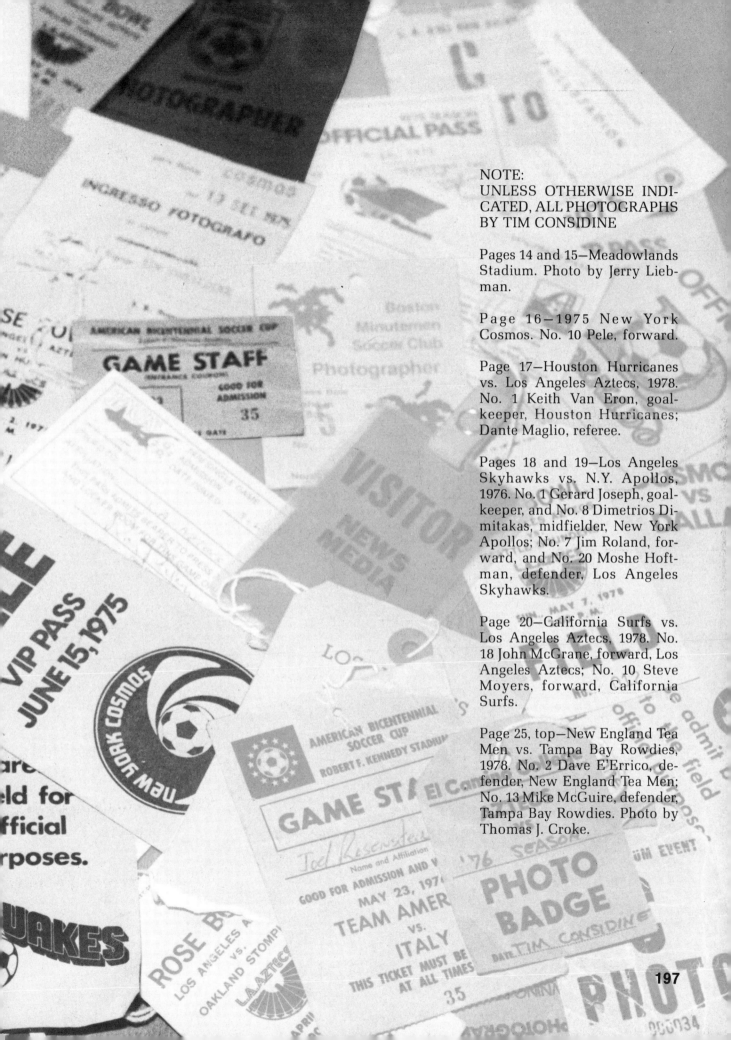

NOTE:
UNLESS OTHERWISE INDICATED, ALL PHOTOGRAPHS BY TIM CONSIDINE

Pages 14 and 15—Meadowlands Stadium. Photo by Jerry Liebman.

Page 16—1975 New York Cosmos. No. 10 Pele, forward.

Page 17—Houston Hurricanes vs. Los Angeles Aztecs, 1978. No. 1 Keith Van Eron, goalkeeper, Houston Hurricanes; Dante Maglio, referee.

Pages 18 and 19—Los Angeles Skyhawks vs. N.Y. Apollos, 1976. No. 1 Gerard Joseph, goalkeeper, and No. 8 Dimetrios Dimitakas, midfielder, New York Apollos; No. 7 Jim Roland, forward, and No. 20 Moshe Hoftman, defender, Los Angeles Skyhawks.

Page 20—California Surfs vs. Los Angeles Aztecs, 1978. No. 18 John McGrane, forward, Los Angeles Aztecs; No. 10 Steve Moyers, forward, California Surfs.

Page 25, top—New England Tea Men vs. Tampa Bay Rowdies, 1978. No. 2 Dave E'Errico, defender, New England Tea Men; No. 13 Mike McGuire, defender, Tampa Bay Rowdies. Photo by Thomas J. Croke.

Page 25, bottom—California Surfs vs. Los Angeles Aztecs, 1978. No. 19 Len Renery, defender, California Surfs; No. 19 Rudy Ybarra, forward, Los Angeles Aztecs.

Page 26—New York Cosmos vs. Los Angeles Aztecs, 1978. No. 8 Bobby McAlinden, forward, Los Angeles Aztecs; No. 6 Franz Beckenbauer, midfielder, New York Cosmos.

Page 21, top—New York Cosmos vs. San Jose Earthquakes, 1975. No. 15 Ramon Mifflin, midfielder, New York Cosmos; No. 8 Johnny Moore, midfielder, and No. 5 Gabbo Gavric, defender, San Jose Earthquakes.

Page 21, bottom—Los Angeles Aztecs vs. Minnesota Kicks, 1977. No. 4 Bernie Fagan, defender, Los Angeles Aztecs; No. 14 Terry Mancini, defender, and No. 16 Ron Futcher, forward, Minnesota Kicks.

Page 22, top—Seattle Sounders vs. Los Angeles Aztecs, 1977. No. 20 Bruce Rudroff, midfielder, Seattle Sounders; No. 5 Charlie Cooke, midfielder, Los Angeles Aztecs.

Page 22, bottom—Oakland Stompers vs. Los Angeles Aztecs, 1978. No. 9 Ron Davies, forward, Los Angeles Aztecs; No. 5 Paki Paunovic, midfielder, and No. 4 Volker Fass, midfielder, Oakland Stompers.

Page 23—San Jose Earthquakes vs. New York Cosmos, 1975. No. 23 Tommy Ord, forward, New York Cosmos; No. 22 Julie Veee, midfielder, and No. 23 Geoff Davies, defender, San Jose Earthquakes.

Page 24—New York Cosmos vs. Los Angeles Aztecs, 1975. No. 10 Pele, forward, New York Cosmos; No. 4 Allan Jones, defender, Los Angeles Aztecs.

Page 27—Los Angeles Aztecs vs. Dallas Tornados, 1978. No. 9 Ron Davies, forward, Los Angeles Aztecs; No. 5 Max Thompson, defender, Dallas Tornados.

Page 28—New York Cosmos vs. Los Angeles Aztecs, 1977. No. 10 Pele, forward, New York Cosmos; No. 14 Julie Veee, midfielder, Los Angeles Aztecs.

Page 29—Los Angeles Aztecs vs. Dallas Tornados, 1976. No. 9 Ron Davies, forward, and No. 7 George Sorjec, forward, Los Angeles Aztecs; No. 21 David Chadwick, forward, Dallas Tornados.

Page 30—Los Angeles Skyhawks vs. Tacoma Tides, 1976. No. 7 Jim Roland, forward, Los Angeles Skyhawks.

Page 31—Los Angeles Aztecs vs. Vancouver Whitecaps, 1976. No. 6 Sam Lenarduzzi, defender, Vancouver Whitecaps; No. 11 George Best, forward, Los Angeles Aztecs.

Pages 32 and 33—Houston Hurricanes vs. Los Angeles Aztecs, 1978. No. 2 Ian Anderson, defender, and No. 26 Nick Megaloudis, defender, Houston Hurricanes; No. 10 Wolfgang Suhnholz, midfielder, Los Angeles Aztecs.

Page 34—California Surfs vs. Toronto Metro-Croatia, 1978. No. 6 Manuel Velazquez, forward, Toronto Metro-Croatia; No. 8 George Graham, defender, and No. 12 Al Trost, midfielder, California Surfs.

Page 35—Los Angeles Aztecs vs. Toronto Metro-Croatia, 1978. No. 2 Bobby Sibbald, defender and No. 4 Tommy Smith, defender, Los Angeles Aztecs; No. 19 Ray Treacy, forward, No. 10 Ivan Poljak, midfielder, and No. 6 Manuel Velazquez, midfielder, Toronto Metro-Croatia.

Pages 36 and 37—New York Cosmos vs. Portland Timbers, 1975. No. 8 Mirko Liveric, forward, No. 10 Pele, forward, No. 2 Barry Mahy, defender, New York Cosmos; Peter Johnson, referee.

Page 38—Toronto Metro-Croatia vs. California Surfs, 1978. No. 1 Zeljko Bilecki, goalkeeper, Toronto Metro-Croatia.

Page 39—Los Angeles Aztecs vs. Seattle Sounders, 1976. No. 11 George Best, forward, Los Angeles Aztecs.

Pages 40 and 41—Tampa Bay Rowdies vs. Los Angeles Aztecs, 1976. No. 13 Stewart Jump, defender, No. 1 Arnold Mauser, goalkeeper, and No. 2 Farrukh Quraishi, defender, Tampa Bay Rowdies; No. 8 Bobby McAlinden, forward, Los Angeles Aztecs.

Page 42—California Surfs vs. Vancouver Whitecaps, 1978. No. 12 Al Trost, midfielder, California Surf.

Page 43—California Surfs vs. Portland Timbers, 1978. Steve Tidland, linesman; Photo by David Keith.

Pages 44 and 45—Los Angeles Aztecs vs. Seattle Sounders, 1976. No. 11 George Best, forward, Los Angeles Aztecs; No. 17 Dave Gillett, defender and No. 16 Adrian Webster, defender, Seattle Sounders.

Pages 46 and 47—New York Cosmos vs. San Jose Earthquakes, 1976. No. 9 Giorgio Chinaglia, forward, New York Cosmos; No. 21 Miroslav Pavlovic, defender, San Jose Earthquakes.

Pages 48 and 49—New York Cosmos vs. Boston Minutemen, 1975. No. 1 Sam Nusum, goalkeeper, New York Cosmos; No. 13 Eusebio, Boston Minutemen.

Page 53—New York Cosmos vs. San Jose Earthquakes, 1975. No. 13 Dave Kemp, defender, San Jose Earthquakes; No. 8 Mirko Liveric, forward, New York Cosmos.

Page 54, top—California Surfs vs. Portland Timbers, 1978. No. 9 Clyde Best, forward, Portland Timbers; No. 19 Len Renery, defender, California Surfs.

Page 54, bottom—California Surfs vs. Portland Timbers, 1978. No. 9 Clyde Best, forward, Portland Timbers; No. 19 Len Renery, defender, California Surfs.

Page 55—New York Cosmos vs. Vancouver Whitecaps, 1975. No. 10 Pele, forward, New York Cosmos; No. 7 Les Wilson, midfielder, Vancouver Whitecaps.

Page 58, top—Los Angeles Aztecs vs. New York Cosmos, 1978. No. 7 Steve David, forward, Los Angeles Aztecs; No. 2 Bobby Smith, defender, and No. 3 Nelsi Morais, defender, New York Cosmos.

Page 58, bottom—New York Cosmos vs. Vancouver Whitecaps, 1975. No. 10 Pele, forward, New York Cosmos; No. 12 Bruce Twamley, defender, and No. 6 Sam Lenarduzzi, defender, Vancouver Whitecaps.

Page 59—New York Cosmos, 1975. No. 10 Pele, forward.

Page 60—Los Angeles Aztecs vs. California Surfs, 1978. No. 9 Dan Counce, forward, California Surfs; No. 18 John McGrane, defender, Los Angeles Aztecs.

Page 61—Los Angeles Aztecs, 1976. No. 11 George Best, forward.

Page 62—Tampa Bay Rowdies, 1977. No. 10 Rodney Marsh, forward, and No. 12 Derek Smethurst, forward, Tampa Bay Rowdies; Peter Johnson, referee; Photo by Rod Millington.

Page 63—Los Angeles Aztecs vs. Vancouver Whitecaps, 1977. No. 8 Bobby McAlinden, forward, Los Angeles Aztecs; No. 5 Bob Lenarduzzi, defender, and No. 4 Holger Osieck, defender, Vancouver Whitecaps.

Page 64, top—Los Angeles Aztecs vs. New York Cosmos, 1976. No. 10 Pele, forward and midfielder, New York Cosmos; No. 15 Jose Lopez, defender, and No. 1 Graham Horn, goalkeeper, Los Angeles Aztecs.

Page 64, bottom—New York Cosmos vs. Roma, 1975. No. 15 Ramon Mifflin, midfielder, New York Cosmos.

Page 65—Los Angeles Aztecs vs. Oakland Stompers, 1978. No. 19 Rudy Ybarra, forward, Los Angeles Aztecs; No. 3 Alec Lindsay, defender, Oakland Stompers.

Page 66—New York Cosmos vs. Portland Timbers, 1975. No. 10 Pele, forward, New York Cosmos.

Page 67—Los Angeles Aztecs vs. Houston Hurricanes, 1978. No. 7 Steve David, forward, Los Angeles Aztecs; No. 26 Nick Megaloudis, defender, Houston Hurricanes.

Page 68, top—New York Cosmos, 1978. No. 3 Nelsi Morais, defender. Photo by David Keith.

Page 68, bottom—Los Angeles Aztecs, 1976. No. 11 George Best, forward.

Page 69, top—Los Angeles Aztecs vs. New York Cosmos, 1976. No. 6 Luis Marotte, midfielder, and No. 9 Ron Davies, forward, Los Angeles Aztecs; No. 10 Pele, forward, No. 9 Giorgio Chinaglia, forward, and No. 5 Keith Eddy, forward, New York Cosmos.

Page 69, bottom—Los Angeles Aztecs vs. New York Cosmos, 1978. No. 11 George Best, forward, and No. 10 Wolfgang Suhnholz, midfielder, Los Angeles Aztecs; No. 14 Terry Garbett, midfielder, No. 4 Werner Roth, defender, No. 1 Erol Yasin, goalkeeper, and No. 3 Nelsi Morais, defender, New York Cosmos.

Pages 70 and 71—Dallas Tornados vs. Los Angeles Aztecs, 1976. No. 1 Ken Cooper, goalkeeper, No. 8 Bobby Hope, midfielder, No. 5 Dick Hall, defender, and No. 11 Kevin Kewley, midfielder, Dallas Tornados; No. 7 George Sorjec, midfielder, Los Angeles Aztecs.

Pages 72 and 73—California Surfs vs. Vancouver Whitecaps, 1978. No. 20 Malcolm Hinton, forward, Vancouver Whitecaps; No. 6 Malcolm Lord, midfielder, and No. 12 Al Trost, midfielder, California Surfs.

Page 74—Los Angeles Aztecs vs. Seattle Sounders, 1977. No. 3 Phil Beal, midfielder, Los Angeles Aztecs; No. 3 Jim McAllister, defender, Seattle Sounders.

Page 75—Los Angeles Aztecs vs. Minnesota Kicks, 1977. No. 9 Ron Davies, forward, Los Angeles Aztecs; No. 18 Ron Futcher, forward, Minnesota Kicks.

Page 76—Los Angeles Aztecs vs. Oakland Stompers, 1978. No. 6 Gary Jones, forward, Los Angeles Aztecs; No. 6 Peter Enders, defender, and No. 18 Bozidar Ban, defender, Oakland Stompers.

Page 77, top—Los Angeles Aztecs vs. New York Cosmos, 1978. No. 8 Bobby McAlinden, midfielder, Los Angeles Aztecs; No. 21 Gary Etherington, forward, and No. 8 Vladislav Bogicevic, midfielder, New York Cosmos.

Page 77, bottom—New York Cosmos vs. Vancouver Whitecaps, 1975. No. 10 Pele, forward, New York Cosmos; No. 7 Les Wilson, midfielder, Vancouver Whitecaps.

Page 78—Los Angeles Aztecs vs. Seattle Sounders, 1978. No. 8 Bobby McAlinden, midfielder, Los Angeles Aztecs; No. 18 Tommy Ord, forward, Seattle Sounders; Hener Landuger, referee.

Page 79—New York Cosmos vs. Roma, 1975. No. 10 Pele, forward, and No. 8 Mirko Liveric, forward, New York Cosmos.

Page 80—New York Cosmos vs. Roma, 1975. No. 8 Mirko Liveric, forward, New York Cosmos.

Page 81, top—California Surfs vs. Tampa Bay Rowdies, 1978. No. 8 Wes McLeod, midfielder, and No. 10 Rodney Marsh, forward, Tampa Bay Rowdies; No. 3 Anselmo Vicioso, forward, No. 9 Dan Counce, forward, No. 14 Chris Dangerfield, midfielder, No. 5 Bob O'Leary, midfielder, No. 12 Al Trost, midfielder, and No. 7 Manuel Cuenca, forward, California Surfs.

Page 82, top—New York Cosmos vs. Roma, 1975. No. 23 Tommy Ord, forward, New York Cosmos.

Page 82, bottom—Los Angeles Aztecs vs. Hawaii, 1977. No. 6 Des Backos, forward, Los Angeles Aztecs.

Page 83—Los Angeles Aztecs vs. Chicago Sting, 1977. No. 1 Billy Mishalow, goalkeeper, Los Angeles Aztecs.

Page 84—Los Angeles Aztecs vs. San Jose Earthquakes, 1977. No. 12 Martin Cohen, midfielder, Los Angeles Aztecs.

Page 85—Ft. Lauderdale Strikers vs. Chicago Sting, 1977. No. 1 Gordon Banks, goalkeeper, No. 3 Ray Lugg, defender, Ft. Lauderdale Strikers; No. 3 Benny Alon, forward, Chicago Sting. Photo by Jon Van Woerden.

Page 86, top—New York Cosmos vs. Los Angeles Aztecs, 1976. No. 9 Giorgio Chinaglia, forward, New York Cosmos; No. 2 Peter Smith, defender, Los Angeles Aztecs.

Page 86, bottom—Los Angeles Aztecs vs. San Jose Earthquakes, 1977. No. 17 Steve David, forward, Los Angeles, Aztecs.

Page 87, top—New York Cosmos vs. Los Angeles Aztecs, 1976. No. 9 Giorgio Chinaglia, forward, New York Cosmos; No. 2 Peter Smith, defender, Los Angeles Aztecs.

Page 87, bottom—Los Angeles Aztecs vs. San Jose Earthquakes, 1977. No. 17 Steve David, forward, Los Angeles Aztecs.

Pages 88 and 89—New York Cosmos vs. St. Louis Stars, 1975. No. 10 Pele, forward, New York Cosmos.

Page 91, bottom—California Surfs vs. Toronto Metro-Croatia, 1978. Toros Kibritjian, referee.

Page 92—Los Angeles Aztecs vs. New York Cosmos, 1978. No. 7 Steve David, forward, Los Angeles Aztecs; John Davies, referee.

Page 93—San Jose Earthquake vs. Tampa Bay Rowdies, 1977. No. 10 Rodney Marsh, midfielder, Tampa Bay Rowdies; No. 13 Dave Kemp, defender, San Jose Earthquakes. Photo by Ray Gouldsberry.

Page 94, top—Los Angeles Aztecs vs. San Antonio Thunder, 1976. No. 8 Bobby McAlinden, forward, Los Angeles Aztecs; No. 12 Pedro Martinez, defender, and No. 4 Ismael Moreira, defender, San Antonio Thunder.

Page 94, bottom—Los Angeles Aztecs vs. San Antonio Thunder, 1976. No. 8 Bobby McAlinden, forward, Los Angeles Aztecs; No. 12 Pedro Martinez, defender, and No. 4 Ismael Moreira, defender, San Antonio Thunder.

Page 95—California Surfs vs. Tampa Bay Rowdies, 1978. No. 9 Dan Counce, forward, California Surfs; No. 8 Wes McLeod, midfielder, and No. 7 Steve Wegerle, forward, Tampa Bay Rowdies.

Page 96—Ft. Lauderdale Strikers vs. Tampa Bay Rowdies, 1977. No. 17 Kevin Eagan, defender, and No. 18 Winston DuBois, goalkeeper, Tampa Bay Rowdies; No. 10 Ronnie Sharp, midfielder, and No. 22 Colin Fowles, midfielder, Ft. Lauderdale Strikers. Photo by Jon Van Woerden.

Page 97—Los Angeles Aztecs vs. Vancouver Whitecaps, 1977. No. 1 Bob Rigby, goalkeeper, and No. 14 Terry Mancini, defender, Los Angeles Aztecs; No. 9 Alan Willey, forward, Minnesota Kicks.

Page 98—Los Angeles Skyhawks vs. Tacoma Tides, 1976. No. 1 Bruce Aarena, goalkeeper, Tacoma Tides.

Page 99, top—Los Angeles Aztecs vs. Vancouver Whitecaps, 1976. No. 15 Daryl Samson, midfielder, No. 3 Bruce Wilson, defender, and No. 5 Bob Lenarduzzi, defender, Vancouver Whitecaps; No. 16 John Mason, midfielder, Los Angeles Aztecs.

Page 99, bottom—New York Cosmos vs. Los Angeles Aztecs, 1976. No. 9 Ron Davies, forward, Los Angeles Aztecs; No. 8 Terry Garbett, midfielder, New York Cosmos.

Page 100—New York Cosmos, 1975. No. 10 Pele, forward.

Page 101, top—New York Cosmos vs. Los Angeles Aztecs, 1976. No. 4 Bernie Fagan, defender, Los Angeles Aztecs; No. 9 Giorgio Chinaglia, forward, New York Cosmos.

Page 101, bottom—California Surfs vs. Portland Timbers, 1978. No. 00 Mike Poole, goalkeeper, No. 10 Ike MacKay, forward, No. 8 Jimmy Conway, midfielder, Portland Timbers; No. 9 Dan Counce, forward, California Surfs.

Page 102—Tampa Bay Rowdies vs. New York Cosmos, 1977. No. 20 Mike Dillon, defender, New York Cosmos; No. 8 Wes McLeod, midfielder, No. 4 Arsene Auguste, defender, No. 3 Jim Fleeting, defender, and No. 7 Steve Wegerle, forward, Tampa Bay Rowdies. Photo courtesy Tampa Bay Rowdies.

Page 103—New York Cosmos vs. San Jose Earthquakes, 1975. No. 8 Mirko Liveric, forward, New York Cosmos; John Davies, referee; Mike Saunders, trainer, New York Cosmos.

Page 104—Toronto Metro-Croatia vs. California Surfs, 1978. No. 8 Ignacio Salcedo, midfielder, Toronto Metro-Croatia; No. 4 Peter Wall, defender, California Surfs.

Page 105, top—Los Angeles Aztecs vs. Rochester Lancers, 1976. No. 11 George Best, forward, Los Angeles Aztecs; No. 21 Meno Droegmiller, goalkeeper, Rochester Lancers.

Page 105, bottom—California Surfs vs. Vancouver Whitecaps, 1978. No. 20 Alan Hinton, forward, and No. 11 Kevin Hector, forward, Vancouver Whitecaps; Enrique Ruvalcaba, linesman.

Page 106—New York Cosmos, 1975. No. 10 Pele, forward.

Page 107—California Surfs vs. Tampa Bay Rowdies, 1978. No. 3 Anselmo Vicioso, forward, No. 7 Manuel Cuenca, forward, and No. 14 Chris Dangerfield, midfielder, California Surfs; No. 7 Steve Wegerle, forward, No. 11 Graham Paddon, midfielder, No. 5 Dave Robb, forward, No. 10 Rodney Marsh, midfielder, and No. 8 Wes McLeod, midfielder, Tampa Bay Rowdies.

Page 108, top—California Surfs vs. Portland Timbers, 1978. Steve Tidland, linesman. Photo by David Keith.

Page 108, bottom—Los Angeles Aztecs vs. Dallas Tornados, 1977. No. 8 Bobby McAlinden, forward, Los Angeles Aztecs; John Greenwood, linesman.

Page 109—New York Cosmos vs. Malmö, Sweden, 1975. No. 22 John Coyne, defender, New York Cosmos.

Page 110—Los Angeles Aztecs vs. Oakland Stompers, 1978. No. 6 Gary Jones, forward, Los Angeles Aztecs; No. 5 Paki Paunovic, midfielder, Oakland Stompers.

Page 111—New York Cosmos vs. Malmö, Sweden, 1975. No. 1 Jan Moller, goalkeeper, Malmö; No. 7 Julio Correa, forward, New York Cosmos.

Pages 114 and 115—California Surfs vs. Portland Timbers, 1978. No. 9 Dan Counce, forward, California Surfs; No. 3 Clive Charles, defender, and No. 10 Ike MacKay, forward, Portland Timbers.

Page 116, top—Los Angeles Aztecs vs. Tampa Bay Rowdies, 1976. No. 11 George Best, forward, Los Angeles Aztecs; No. 19 Lenny Glover, midfielder, Tampa Bay Rowdies.

Page 116, bottom—New York Cosmos vs. San Jose Earthquakes, 1975. No. 10 Pele, forward, New York Cosmos; No. 1 Mike Ivanow, goalkeeper, and No. 23 Geoff Davies, defender, San Jose Earthquakes.

Page 117, top—Los Angeles Aztecs vs. New York Cosmos, 1977. No. 3 Phil Beal, defender, and No. 1 Bobby Rigby, goalkeeper, Los Angeles Aztecs; No. 20 Mike Dillon, defender, and No. 9 Giorgio Chinaglia, forward, New York Cosmos. Photo by Willie Hunt.

Page 119, top—Tacoma Tides vs. Los Angeles Skyhawks, 1976. No. 2 Alty McKenzie, defender, Los Angeles Skyhawks; No. 1 Bruce Aarena, goalkeeper, Tacoma Tides.

Page 119, bottom—New York Cosmos vs. San Jose Earthquakes, 1976. No. 10 Pele, forward, New York Cosmos; No. 19 Antonio Simoes, midfielder, San Jose Earthquakes.

Pages 120 and 121—California Surfs vs. Tampa Bay Rowdies, 1978. No. 18 Andy McBride, defender, and No. 5 Bob O'Leary, defender, California Surfs; No. 10 Rodney Marsh, forward, Tampa Bay Rowdies.

Page 122, top—New York Cosmos vs. Los Angeles Aztecs, 1978. No. 7 Steve David, forward, Los Angeles Aztecs; No. 14 Nelsi Morais, defender, New York Cosmos.

Page 122, bottom—New York Cosmos vs. Los Angeles Aztecs, 1978. No. 7 Steve David, forward, Los Angeles Aztecs; No. 14 Nelsi Morais, defender, New York Cosmos.

Page 123—Los Angeles Aztecs vs. Houston Hurricanes, 1978. No. 13 Stewart Jump, defender, Houston Hurricanes; No. 8 Bobby McAlinden, midfielder, Los Angeles Aztecs.

Pages 124 and 125—San Jose Earthquakes vs. New York Cosmos, 1976. No. 9 Giorgio Chinaglia, forward, New York Cosmos; No. 14 John Rowlands, defender, and No. 24 Mike Hewitt, goalkeeper, San Jose Earthquakes.

Page 126—New York Cosmos vs. Sweden, 1975. No. 17 Brian Rowan, defender, New York Cosmos.

Page 127—Los Angeles Aztecs vs. Dallas Tornados, 1976. No. 21 Dave Chadwick, forward, Dallas Tornados; No. 9 Ron Davies, forward, No. 16 John Mason, midfielder, and No. 11 George Best, forward, Los Angeles Aztecs.

Page 128, top—New York Cosmos vs. Dallas Tornados, 1975. No. 18 Richard Reynolds, forward, Dallas Tornados; No. 1 Sam Nusum, goalkeeper, New York Cosmos.

Page 128, bottom—New York Cosmos vs. Dallas Tornados, 1975. No. 18 Richard Reynolds, forward, Dallas Tornados; No. 1 Sam Nusum, goalkeeper, New York Cosmos.

Page 130—Los Angeles Aztecs vs. Seattle Sounders, 1977. No. 14 Terry Mancini, defender, Los Angeles Aztecs; No. 1 Tony Chursky, goalkeeper, No. 20 Bruce Ridcoff, defender, and No. 4 Gordon Wallace, midfielder, Seattle Sounders.

Page 131—California Surfs vs. Tampa Bay Rowdies, 1978. No. 21 Dave Jokerst, goalkeeper, California Surfs; No. 11 Graham Paddon, midfielder, Tampa Bay Rowdies.

Page 132—New York Cosmos vs. Stockholmes-Alliansen, 1975. No. 23 Luis de la Fuente, defender, New York Cosmos; No. 5 Tommy Berggren, defender, Stockholmes-Alliansen.

Page 132, bottom—Los Angeles Aztecs vs. New York Cosmos, 1978. No. 8 Vladislav Bogicevic, midfielder, New York Cosmos; No. 15 Ramon Mifflin, midfielder, Los Angeles Aztecs.

Page 133—New York Cosmos vs. Vancouver Whitecaps, 1975. No. 9 Brian Budd, forward, and No. 7 Buzz Parsons, forward, Vancouver Whitecaps; No. 10 Pele, forward, New York Cosmos.

Page 134, top—California Surfs vs. Los Angeles Aztecs, 1978. No. 7 Steve David, forward, and No. 10 Wolfgang Suhnholz, midfielder, Los Angeles Aztecs; No. 9 Dan Counce, forward, and No. 8 George Graham, midfielder, California Surfs; Dante Naglio, referee.

Page 134, bottom—referee emblem.

Page 135—New York Cosmos vs. Sweden, 1975. No. 10 Pele, forward, and No. 17 Brian Rowan, defender, New York Cosmos.

Page 136, top—New York Apollos, 1976. No. 1 Gerard Joseph, goalkeeper.

Page 136, bottom—Los Angeles Aztecs vs. San Jose Earthquakes, 1977. No. 24 Mike Hewitt, goalkeeper, and No. 2 Buzz Demling, defender, San Jose Earthquakes; No. 7 Steve David, forward, Los Angeles Aztecs.

Page 137, top—Los Angeles Aztecs vs. Dallas Tornados, 1976. No. 7 George Sorjic, forward, Los Angeles Aztecs; No. 3 George Ley, defender, and No. 1 Ken Cooper, goalkeeper, Dallas Tornados.

Page 137, bottom—Los Angeles Skyhawks vs. New York Apollos, 1976. No. 6 Louis Speranza, midfielder, No. 2 Peter Christoforides, defender, and No. 1 Gerard Joseph, goalkeeper, New York Apollos; No. 9 Jim Hinch, forward, Los Angeles Skyhawks.

Page 138, top—New York Cosmos, 1975. No. 10 Pele, forward.

Page 138, bottom—Los Angeles Aztecs vs. San Antonio Thunder, 1976. No. 6 Bobby Moore, defender, No. 4 Pedro Martinez, defender, San Antonio Thunder.

Page 139—Los Angeles Aztecs vs. Oakland Stompers, 1978. No. 6 Gary Jones, forward, Los Angeles Aztecs; No. 2 Joe Raduka, defender, Oakland Stompers.

Page 140—Los Angeles Aztecs vs. New York Cosmos, 1976. No. 11 George Best, forward, Los Angeles Aztecs; No. 3 Brian Rowan, defender, New York Cosmos.

Page 141—Los Angeles Aztecs vs. San Antonio Thunder, 1976. No. 12 George Best, forward, Los Angeles Aztecs; No. 6 Bobby Moore, defender, San Antonio Thunder.

Pages 142 and 143—Los Angeles Aztecs vs. Chicago Sting, 1977. No. 7 Steve David, forward, Los Angeles Aztecs; No. 1 Mervyn Cawston, goalkeeper, and No. 10 John Kowalik, forward, Chicago Sting.

Page 144—Los Angeles Aztecs vs. San Jose Earthquakes, 1976. No. 11 George Best, forward, Los Angeles Aztecs; No. 13 Dave Kemp, defender, San Jose Earthquakes.

Page 145—Los Angeles Aztecs vs. New York Cosmos, 1978. No. 8 Bobby McAlinden, midfielder, and No. 5 Charlie Cook, midfielder, Los Angeles Aztecs; No. 5 Carlos Alberto, defender, and No. 6 Franz Beckenbauer, midfielder, New York Cosmos.

Page 146—New York Cosmos vs. Rochester Lancers, 1975. No. 10 Pele, forward, New York Cosmos; No. 14 George Lamptey, defender, Vancouver Whitecaps.

Page 147—California Surfs vs. Los Angeles Aztecs, 1978. No. 10 Steve Moyers, forward, and No. 9 Dan Counce, midfielder, California Surfs; No. 5 Charlie Cook, midfielder, and No. 11 George Best, forward, Los Angeles Aztecs.

Page 148—Los Angeles Aztecs vs. Seattle Sounders, 1977. No. 9 Ron Davies, forward, Los Angeles Aztecs; No. 5 Mike England, defender, Seattle Sounders.

Page 149—Los Angeles Aztecs vs. Las Vegas Quicksilvers, 1977. No. 9 Ron Davies, forward, Los Angeles Aztecs; No. 12 Tom Glatti, defender, Las Vegas Quicksilvers.

Page 150—Los Angeles Aztecs vs. San Antonio Thunder, 1976. No. 11 George Best, forward, Los Angeles Aztecs; No. 6 Bobby Moore, defender, No. 12 Tom Callaghan, midfielder, San Antonio Thunder.

Page 151—Los Angeles Aztecs vs. San Jose Earthquakes, 1977. No. 2 Buzz Demling, defender, and No. 12 Leroy DeLeon, forward, San Jose Earthquakes; No. 6 Des Backos, forward, Los Angeles Aztecs.

Pages 152 and 153—California Surfs vs. Portland Timbers, 1978. No. 8 George Graham, midfielder, and No. 18 Andy McBride, defender, California Surfs; No. 4 Mike Hobin, defender, and No. 9 Clyde Best, forward, Portland Timbers.

Page 154—New York Cosmos vs. Stockholms-Alliansen, 1975. No. 10 Pele, forward, New York Cosmos; No. 3 Thom Ahlund, defender, Stockholms-Alliansen.

Page 155, top—Los Angeles Aztecs vs. New York Cosmos, 1978. No. 11 George Best, forward, Los Angeles Aztecs; No. 6 Franz Beckenbauer, midfielder, and No. 2 Bobby Smith, defender, New York Cosmos.

Page 155, bottom—Los Angeles Aztecs vs. New York Cosmos, 1978. No. 11 George Best, forward, Los Angeles Aztecs; No. 6 Franz Beckenbauer, midfielder, and No. 2 Bobby Smith, defender, New York Cosmos.

Pages 156 and 157—Los Angeles Skyhawks vs. New York Apollos, 1976. No. 2 Peter Christoforides, defender, No. 6 Louis Speranza, midfielder, Los Angeles Skyhawks; No. 16 Dave Power, forward, New York Apollos.

Page 158—California Surfs vs. Vancouver Whitecaps, 1978. No. 6 Malcolm Lord, midfielder, California Surfs; No. 14 Steve Kimber, midfielder, Vancouver Whitecaps.

Page 159—New York Cosmos vs. Rochester Lancers, 1975. No. 10 Pele, forward, New York Cosmos; No. 2 Craig Reynolds, defender, Rochester Lancers.

Page 160—San Jose Earthquakes vs. New York Cosmos, 1975. No. 2 Buzz Dembling, defender, San Jose Earthquakes; No. 7 Julio Correa, forward, New York Cosmos.

Page 161, top—California Surfs vs. Portland Timbers, 1978. No. 19 Len Renery, defender, California Surfs; No. 9 Clyde Best, forward, Portland Timbers.

Page 161, bottom—California Surfs vs. Portland Timbers, 1978. No. 19 Len Renery, defender, California Surfs; No. 9 Clyde Best, forward, Portland Timbers.

Page 163—Los Angeles Aztecs vs. Minnesota Kicks, 1977. No. 16 Ron Futcher, forward, Minnesota Kicks; No. 16 John Mason, midfielder, Los Angeles Aztecs.

Pages 164 and 165—Tampa Bay Rowdies vs. California Surfs, 1978. No. 8 Wes McLeod, forward, No. 11 Graham Paddon, midfielder, and No. 10 Rodney Marsh, midfielder, Tampa Bay Rowdies; No. 7 Manuel Cuenca, forward, No. 9 Dan Counce, forward, No. 12 Al Trost, midfielder, No. 6 Malcolm Lord, midfielder, and No. 14 Chris Dangerfield, midfielder, California Surfs.

Page 166—New York Cosmos vs. Norway, 1975. No. 10 Pele, forward, New York Cosmos.

Page 167, top—California Surfs vs. Portland Timbers, 1978. No. 10 Ike McKay, forward, Portland Timbers; No. 9 Dan Counce, forward, California Surfs.

Page 167, bottom—California Surfs vs. Portland Timbers, 1978; No. 10 Ike McKay, forward, Portland Timbers; No. 9 Dan Counce, forward, California Surfs.

Page 167—New York Cosmos Vs. San Jose Earthquakes, 1976. No. 3 Laurie Calloway, defender, San Jose Earthquakes; Redge Clark, referee.

Milestones in American Soccer

1860s—Soccer is introduced to the United States by British sailors and businessmen.

1904—The Greater Los Angeles Soccer League is formed. The GLASL is the oldest existing soccer league in the United States.

1904—The St. Rose team of St. Louis represents the United States at the Olympics and is defeated by Canada, 4-0.

1905—The first International Collegiate Association is formed and the Ivy League joins.

1913—The United States Soccer Association (formerly the United States Soccer Football Association) joins the Federation of International Football Associations.

1930—The United States qualifies for the first World Cup.
• defeats Belgium, 3-0, in the first round
• defeats Paraguay, 3-0, in the second round
• loses to Argentina, 6-1, in the semifinals

1930—The American Soccer League is founded.

1934—The United States qualifies for the World Cup again, but is defeated by the eventual winner, Italy, in the first round.

1950—The United States qualifies for the World Cup and defeats cofavorite England in the first round. This victory is still considered one of the most sensational upsets in the history of international soccer. The United States has not qualified for the World Cup since.

1967—Two unsuccessful pro leagues merge to become the North American Soccer League.

1970—The American Soccer League (the older of the two leagues in the United States) expands to the West Coast and now consists of ten teams.

1975—Pele plays his first game as a New York Cosmo.

1977—August 14—a record 77,691 people attended a Cosmos-Ft. Lauderdale game.

1977—October 1—Pele plays his last game.